Dedication

I dedicate this book to "John," my mentor and friend who had no body; without him, the subtle worlds would have remained a mystery to me.

I dedicate this book to my wife, Julie, my daily companion in inner work, without whom that work would be lonely indeed; spiritual allies can do many things but they can't give you a cuddle when you need it.

I dedicate this book to my children, who came to us from the subtle worlds and who give my work a future.

I dedicate this book to all the colleagues and fellow teachers I've know over the years who have valued my inner contacts and given me needed support, peer review and honest reflection.

And I dedicate this book to all of you who have honored me by participating in my classes. You have given me the opportunity and enabled me to find the words to let my explorations of the subtle worlds live in the world.

Acknowledgements

A book is always the product of many minds, many hearts, and many hands. If it takes a village to "raise a child," it certainly takes one to bring a book into reality. I want to acknowledge and thank those who made this book possible. Chief among those is my wife, Julie. She not only is my inspiration in my work and my bedrock support when things get rough, she is also my main editor who gives my prose more sparkle and clarity than it would have otherwise. It's not for nothing she's taught all those creative writing classes.

I want to acknowledge my partners in Lorian, Jeremy Berg and Freya Secrest, without whom this book would probably never see the light of day. I could not ask for better friends or colleagues. This is especially true as Jeremy is my publisher as well as my friend. Thanks, Jeremy, for always being there to give good advice when I got stuck with the writing. Your wise vision got me through the times when I had lost my own vision for the book and had gotten stuck. And thank you for the outstanding cover!

When I'm able, I ask friends to read my manuscripts in advance and give me comments on what works and what doesn't. Freya has always been one of my best readers. But with this book, there are two others who made significant contributions and at a critical juncture helped me revision the direction the book was going and thus made it a very much better document than it would have been otherwise.

Thank you very much to my friends Claire Blatchford, a most excellent writer of spiritual books herself, and Susan Stanton Rotman, an intuitive counselor of great wisdom and skill. Both of these women have worked with the subtle worlds for many years and are familiar with its ins and outs.

I want to thank all those who have participated in my classes, particularly those that have dealt with forming partnerships with

Subtle Worlds

An Explorer's
Field Notes

David Spangler

Subtle Worlds:
An Explorer's Field Notes

Edited by Julia Spangler and Freya Secrest
Book Design by Jeremy Berg
Cover Photos from istockphoto

Published by Lorian Press
2204 E Grand Ave.
Everett, WA 98201

ISBN-10: 0-936878-26-6
ISBN-13: 978-0-936878-26-3

Spangler/David
Subtle Worlds: An Explorer's Field Notes /David Spangler

First Edition January 2010

Printed in the United States of America

0 9 8 7 6 5 4 3 2 1

www.lorian.org

the inner worlds and with spiritual allies. Over the years you have encouraged and helped me put words to my experiences that otherwise I might never have talked about, much less written a book about.

And finally—and very far from least—I wish to acknowledge and thank my non-physical allies and colleagues. You are truly in many ways my co-authors and co-creators for this book. May it further your dreams of a world and a humanity restored to wholeness.

Table of Contents

Introduction

I have been engaged with the non-physical dimensions of the earth all of my life. It is not unusual for a child to have perceptions and awareness of this other reality. Children are, after all, newly arrived immigrants from the realms of spirit, and the knowledge of their origin is closer to the surface. But in our culture at least, it *is* unusual for that perception to last and develop. Our culture in general neither understands nor supports it, viewing it as imagination at best and delusion at worst. In the face of a lack of understanding or even active disapproval and mockery, the capacity for inner perception is suppressed and lost.

But in my case, I was fortunate that my parents were supportive. While not psychic or clairvoyant themselves, my parents still accepted that there was more to life than just what we could see, hear or feel and accepted that there were realms beyond this one. That their son might have an awareness of these realms was surprising—to my knowledge, there is no history of "second sight" or of feyness in my ancestry—but they took it in their stride, seeing it as a natural capacity that would either disappear with time or develop in its own organic way.

It did develop over time, and when I was twenty, I came into a partnership with a non-physical being whom I called John. He became my mentor, friend, and colleague for twenty-seven years, the first five of which were an intensive training in working with the subtle realms. I tell the story of meeting John and the training that ensued in my book *Apprenticed to Spirit*. This training and partnership created the foundation for my work which over the years has been to conduct research into the nature of the relationships between the subtle worlds and our own and in particular into the nature and processes of incarnation.

Because I grew up with the nonphysical dimensions as part of my everyday life, I came to see them as a natural part of the world, as much a part of the environment of the world as the grass and trees, mountains and skies I see out my window. I have always had a love of biology and chemistry and in college was working towards a degree in molecular biology. I carried this love and perspective over into my work with John and his colleagues. Rather than seeing the subtle worlds in religious or spiritual ways, I have always seen them as earth's "second ecology" and have approached them like a naturalist exploring the wilderness. The classes I have offered, the lectures I've given, and the books I've written over the years have all in one way or another come from this approach and represent reports or field notes from my observations and explorations. That is why I call the chapters in this book "Field Notes."

I have always offered these reports as one person's perceptions and observations, not as some kind of revealed truth. The non-physical worlds represent an environment much larger and more diverse than anything we know on earth. As one person, I can only explore a very tiny part of it. Even that is seen through the lens of my own character and methodologies. Still, I offer what I can in the hopes it will be helpful to others.

In this book I hope to give you a glimpse of the larger wholeness and nature of these worlds and also give you some suggestions about how you can, if you wish, begin your own explorations. This book does not offer an in-depth look at the subtle worlds and the beings upon them; my intent is for it to be an introduction, not a text book. But I do hope that it helps to dispel some of the fear and glamour that surrounds the phenomenon of subtle awareness and contact with non-physical beings.

I have a larger purpose as well. This is the same purpose that brought John into my life in the first place. The earth is not really two worlds, one physical and one non-physical. It is one whole, living system. Yet the separation between these two domains in our own consciousnesses and human activities makes the expression of this wholeness and its potentials difficult. We act as partial people imposing our partiality upon the world, which cannot help but create fragmentation and disharmony. It's as if we try to play a glorious Beethoven piano sonata with one hand tied behind our back. The result leaves much to be desired.

This is the condition that John was particularly concerned about. The purpose of our partnership from the beginning was to explore how to overcome this partiality and express wholeness. Engaging with the subtle worlds isn't simply to experience or explore the non-physical dimensions. The larger purpose is to engage the underlying wholeness that ties the physical and non-physical domains into a living, creative oneness.

John came to me as a representative of a vast spiritual impulse within the subtle worlds towards restoration and wholeness, both within individuals and within the world. In the training he offered me, the emphasis was always on this wholeness. It might be expressed in different ways: as the importance of integration or of personal sovereignty, of collaboration and partnership, and always as the vital, essential nature of love. But the overriding question was always, "How does this contribute to wholeness—the wholeness of a person, the wholeness of a partnership, the wholeness of humanity, or the wholeness of the world.

I bring this same emphasis to this book. I'm not writing about psychic phenomenon, becoming clairvoyant, or receiving guidance, though such skills and experiences might emerge when one engages with the deeper aspects of one's nature. Instead, I hope these field notes and observations from my own explorations will help revision and renew the relationship between ourselves and the non-physical realms that over time has become diminished from the full co-creative collaboration that it could be. We need to set about reclaiming our sacred citizenship in a community of life and consciousness that includes but is not limited to physical existence.

Subtle Worlds:

4

Field Notes One:
An Overview

For some of my readers, the non-physical worlds and the beings who come from them to work with us will be as familiar as your everyday surroundings and friends. But for others, perhaps most, this will be fairly new territory. So what do I mean when I talk about the non-physical realms? Who are the beings who inhabit them?

When most people think about non-physical beings, I have found, the most common assumption is that they are either angels or the ghosts or spirits of dead people; sometimes the two are lumped together under the assumption that we become angels when we die. The other common category is demons or evil spirits roaming the unseen worlds waiting to pounce on and possess unwary human beings. If a person is familiar with fairy tales and mythology, he or she may also acknowledge that non-physical beings may include "nature spirits," spoken of in folklore as faeries, elves, gnomes, and the "Little People," as well as spirits of places such as rivers, mountains, valleys, and the like. I hope to show in this book that non-physical beings are as diverse as the physical life forms that fill our earth. Physical life ranges from single-celled microbes (who are, by the way, the most abundant of all creatures on our world, forming by far and away the bulk of the biomass of the planet) to the great whales, from tiny fungi to towering redwoods. If anything, life seems to me even more varied and wondrous on the inner worlds. To see the non-physical realms as comprised only of human spirits and angels, with perhaps some darker forces and some nature beings thrown in, is like saying the earth only has human beings and trees, with some flies and flowers here and there.

The ecology of the earth is a collection of interrelated

ecosystems, from the very small to the very large, each defined by a set of relationships and interactions between a group of organisms and their environment. That is also how one could describe the various realms that make up the non-physical dimensions: they are a collection of interrelated environments comprised of energy, life, and consciousness. It's why I think of them as earth's "Second Ecology."

Calling them the "non-physical worlds" tells us what they're not—they're not made up of physical, corporeal matter—but doesn't really tell us what they are. One reason modern Western culture dismisses the existence of these realms is not that they are invisible— science deals with lots of things we can't see or hear with unaided senses—but that they are not made of matter. A materialist will say that nothing can exist that is not made of matter in one form or another (and remember, as Einstein proved, energy is another form of matter and vice versa).

Actually, I agree with this. For something to exist, whether it's a rock, a potato, a ferret, a human being, a nature spirit, or an angel, it must have substance. The issue, of course, is what this substance is made of. Clearly, the matter that forms the subtle worlds is not one made up of physical atoms and molecules, or even of subatomic particles. So what is it made up of and how does it relate to our world?

There are plenty of theories and ideas that have been put forward by religious, mystical, philosophical, and esoteric traditions over the centuries. The general consensus is that underlying all phenomena of any kind is a primal substance variously identified as God, the Void, Light, Infinite Mind, Consciousness, Spirit, or the Ground of Being. This is certainly the image that I have gotten over the years from different non-physical contacts.

This primal substance is alive, active, sentient, and generative. Whatever we call it, it differentiates and manifests itself in many ways; physical matter is the product of one such differentiation, whereas the various subtle realms represent other differentiations. A metaphor for this is the electromagnetic spectrum which is made up of electromagnetic radiation at varying wavelengths and frequencies.

What we call the visible light spectrum, made up of the familiar colors of the rainbow, is only a very small fraction of this entire spectrum which ranges from below the wavelength of radio at the long end (the longest waves being limited only by the size of the universe itself) to gamma rays and even shorter at the other end (the shortest waves being tiny fractions of the size of an atom). If you tune into this spectrum at one point, you get microwaves, at another point you get visible colors, while at still a third point, you get x-rays.

The primal substance extends across an infinite and continuous spectrum like this, manifesting various "wavelengths" or "frequencies" of life and sentiency. The physical universe we see every day is one of these many possible wavelengths of beingness. The non-physical worlds are others. And just as the "physical wavelength" manifests in a nearly infinite diversity of forms and expressions, so this is true of the worlds existing on the "subtle" or "non-physical" wavelengths as well. They are vast, diverse and for the most part beyond human comprehension, at least at our present stage of consciousness development.

The point is that at the heart of all things is a generative mystery, something indefinable and indescribable, which is the substance from which all other manifestations of matter arise. And it's important to remember that this primal substance is alive and sentient, containing the qualities and potentials that make life and consciousness as we know them possible, as well as other forms of life and consciousness that we may not yet recognize or be familiar with.

It has been my experience that for those who live in the various non-physical worlds, their environments are as solid and real to them as ours is to us; indeed, I have been told more than once (and have seen for myself) that for them our world is the one that is wispy, immaterial and insubstantial! The characteristics of their environments are almost always very different from what we are used to. Yet like the sea and the land, there is a threshold, a "beach," where subtle matter touches physical matter and the two worlds connect. A quantum physicist friend of mine who has thought deeply about these things once suggested to me that this threshold may well be at the level of quantum interaction. This may well be, but experientially, this threshold exists in a manner accessible to our thoughts and emotions. We carry part of this "beach" within us. This is what makes contact with the unseen worlds possible. It also means that often these contacts may register within us like our own thoughts and feelings, making discernment difficult without practice and leading to the common conclusion that such experiences are all in our heads and that we are "making them up."

This is a very simplified picture, of course, but this is not a book on esoteric cosmology or philosophy. There is a rich esoteric and mystical literature that explores the nature of non-physical matter; it's certainly not as if people have not been thinking about this for a long time, and many interesting insights have arisen from their contemplations and investigations. For further exploration along these lines you might check out authors like Rudolf Steiner, Alice Bailey, Dion Fortune, and R. J. Stewart.

Whatever the substance of the non-physical worlds may be, people have been interacting with them in a variety of ways throughout human history. In this relationship, they have called these realms many things; subtle worlds, inner worlds, the Other Worlds, the spiritual realms, and the unseen worlds are just a few of the names. In my field notes, to provide some variation in writing, I use the subtle worlds, the unseen worlds, and the non-physical worlds interchangeably. I will also refer to them as earth's "second ecology" and as a "subtle ecology."

I also call them the "inner worlds," but I want to explain that phrase. In this case *inner* has nothing to do with a direction. It does not mean that these realms are inside the physical world or inside us. Instead, it means that the senses or capacities used to perceive the subtle worlds are inside us; they are not "outer" physical organs of perception like our eyes or ears. The real meaning of *inner worlds*, then, is "worlds seen through inward means."

The term "spiritual worlds" is often used in reference to these non-physical realms, but I don't do so. I find it problematic. The challenge arises from the two different ways the word *spiritual* is defined and used.

On the one hand, "spiritual" can mean immaterial, incorporeal, and non-physical. That is certainly a good designation for the subtle realms, for that is precisely what they are, at least in comparison to our own everyday world. But "spiritual" is also used to mean holy, sacred, and pertaining to Spirit, which is a description of a quality or set of qualities. It means the presence of something that enhances, nourishes and enlarges life, consciousness, wholeness, wellbeing, and the expression of sacredness. There are certainly places and inhabitants of the subtle worlds who are spiritual in this way, just as there are physical places and people that could be called spiritual as well. But there are places and beings that are not. To simply call the subtle realms "spiritual" is to imply that all manifestations of those realms are radiant and filled with spirit, enhancing and blessing life and consciousness and providing a link to the Sacred. This is not true, and confusing these two uses and meanings of the word "spiritual" can lead to errors of discernment when dealing with the subtle worlds.

If by "spiritual" we mean a part of the Spirit and sacredness that is the ultimate primal substance of creation, then all beings are spiritual in origin and in their essential nature. If by "spiritual" we mean someone who embodies sacred qualities and acts in loving, compassionate and wise ways for the benefit of all, then we know that all beings do not act in this manner. Although every person has the capacity to be spiritual in this sense, we know that many, if not most, people as they go through their day do not do so. This does not mean they are evil, "dark," or negative. It only means they are in the moment self-absorbed, or following a limited agenda, or simply not connecting to a larger wholeness either within themselves or in the world around them. Or they may simply not know how to connect with others in a meaningful and spiritual way. It takes awareness, attention, love, knowledge, and openness to express our spiritual radiance to each other, and sometimes we just aren't manifesting those qualities or may not know how to in the moment. The same is true for many inhabitants of the subtle realms as well.

And just as there are in our world places where the land, the water, or the air has become polluted and toxic and just as there are individuals whose dysfunctional nature has rendered them harmful, such places and individuals unfortunately exist in the inner worlds as well. If I think that all the subtle worlds and all non-physical beings are harmless, helpful and benign—in other words, "spiritual"—I can naively open myself to dangers that I would be wise to avoid. I'll have more to say about this in later field notes.

There *are* beings and places within the subtle ecology that are truly spiritual in every way we may think of. Connecting with such beings and places is always uplifting, inspiring, and filled with blessing. It is those beings and places specifically that I shall refer to as spiritual beings or spiritual realms in the context of this book.

However, it's important to recognize that any being on any level, including the physical, can at any time act in spiritual and sacred ways, with kindness, love, and blessing. In this sense, *spiritual* denotes a potentially universal attribute not limited to certain entities or individuals or certain realms or places. It is a function of a specific relationship with the sacredness at the core of all things and of those actions or expressions that bring sacredness into play in the moment. We all have the capacity to do this at any time if we so choose.

Here's a final word about nomenclature. I use *realm, world, domain,* and *dimension* interchangeably too, to designate different areas of non-physical life and activity. If I took a biological or ecological slant, I could call them "niches" or "bioregions" (or more accurately, I suppose, "psycho-regions" or "nous-regions" from the Greek word *nous* for "mind"). The point is that the non-physical world is not a single, monolithic environment, any more than the physical earth is. We have seas and land, mountains and valley, deserts and jungles, plains and swamps, cities and villages, all with their own native inhabitants and characteristics. The inner worlds are just as diverse, if not more so. So I talk about these areas as "worlds" or "domains" or "realms," but the words mean the same thing, like talking about the "realm of New York City" or the "world of New York City."

However, it is possible to use these words in more precise ways to designate certain specific characteristics and differences between different regions in the subtle world. If I do so in my field notes, I'll let you know when that time comes so there is no confusion.

In my experience, the subtle realms are vast, much larger than the physical world itself, and, more importantly, the natural laws that govern their structure and composition are very different from those that shape our earthly reality. Think of the often confusing and changing landscape in a dream and you get a faint idea of the mutability of some of these inner worlds. They are not chaotic, but they can appear so to an earthly mind used to landscapes and structures that change slowly over time and maintain consistency of form.

An analogy is that of the European explorers in the eighteenth and nineteenth century who investigated the mysterious African continent. Depending on where they went, some found vast deserts while others found dense, lush jungles. Some encountered pygmy people and others tall warriors. Some places resembled the European landscape and others were so different that they might have been on another planet. Which was the "true" description of Africa? Was it desert? Was it jungle? Was it a home to little people or to giants? Of course, all these descriptions were true depending on where you went and what you saw. The same is true for the subtle worlds. Contradictory descriptions can still fit as "bioregions" within a vast ecology.

In my own experience, the subtle worlds form a continuum of life and consciousness. Think of a guitar string. It is a single string yet from it many different notes can be produced. Each subtle realm is one of these notes, possessing a distinct energy signature, its own "sound," so to speak. The differences between these notes constitute the boundaries between the various subtle realms, and of course, between the subtle worlds and the physical, which itself may be considered a "note" on this string. It's also true, and very importantly so, that no note is further away or closer to the string itself than any other; all notes are manifestations of the one string. In an analogous way, no world, whether physical or non-physical, is closer to the Sacred or to the Ground of Being, the Generative Mystery, than any other.

The wonderful nature of consciousness is that it can move up and down the string, just as the fingers of a guitarist move up and down the guitar string or the voice of a singer can move up and down the scales. There is a common and familiar range of notes that we accept as normal, everyday consciousness. This is usually a three-note harmonic blending the physical, the mental and the emotional sides of our nature. But our consciousness can attune to other notes, other frequencies and vibrations of energy, and when we do, we become aware of the subtle worlds.

There are boundaries and thresholds that create distinct zones (the "notes") along this continuum of life and sentiency. Some of these boundaries are flexible and permeable, rather like the boundaries that exist between individual States in the United States. These political boundaries are generally not visible in the landscape itself (though some are, like the Columbia River that divides Oregon from Washington), but they perform a function and have an effect in how human beings conduct their economic, social and political lives. Other boundaries are like mountains and oceans that demark a definite change, a threshold of transformation and metamorphosis, moving from one distinct state of being to another.

The boundary between the realms with which we are most familiar is death, the transformative threshold between the physical and non-physical worlds.

In my experience, these metamorphic boundaries divide the subtle worlds into many varied zones, each with its own relationship to the physical realm and to each other. But for simplicity's sake, I think of there being three primary zones: the incarnational realms, the transitional realm, and the higher-order realms. The difference between them is this. The incarnational realms, which are made up of physical, emotional, mental, and vital or *etheric* manifestations of primal substance, are basically organized around three dimensions of being (four if we include time, as in Einstein's formulation of spacetime). The higher order realms are those that are organized around more than three (or four) dimensions of being; they are *hyperdimensional* and inhabit (or manifest) space and time very differently than we do. Again, think of the difference between the linearity of time and space that we experience in waking everyday life and the fluidity and non-linearity of time and space that we experience in dreams.

There are other differences as well which can make direct contact between the incarnate realms (our world) and the higher-order worlds difficult and challenging, and at times not even possible. Here's a metaphor. When I first went to Britain many years ago, I fried my American-made electric shaver when I plugged it in because I didn't realize there was a difference in current. American electrical devices are designed to run on 110 volts while in Britain the electrical mains deliver 240 volts. That 130 volt differential is what killed my shaver. Next time I had a transformer that "stepped down" the current coming from the British plugs to a level my American shaver could tolerate and use.

Contact with the inner worlds always involves an energy exchange across a differential. Sometimes the energy difference is slight but sometimes it is significant. There is a need for something to bridge that difference so both sides can connect and neither be harmed.

Or to use a less electrical metaphor, imagine a businessman from America attempting to do business in a very different culture, such as that of China or Japan. There are linguistic and cultural differences that can bring about misunderstanding and ruin the deal. For that matter, one need not look to such extreme differences. Again when I was first visiting Britain, I tried to get cookies to go with my tea. In restaurant after restaurant I would ask for cookies only to be told they didn't have any. But then I spied a waiter serving tea and cookies to another patron. Pointing at them, I said to my waiter, "I want some of those." "Oh," he said, "you mean *biscuits!*'

One can think of the higher-order worlds as linguistically and culturally very different from the incarnate realms we live in. Like the American businessman in Japan, we would benefit from the intercession of someone familiar and adept in both cultures, someone who can translate and bridge the differences.

For this reason, there is an intermediate realm that can mediate between the physical, incarnate worlds and the higher-order worlds, enabling them to connect in beneficial ways. I call this the transitional realm. It's quite possible for an individual to learn how to perform this transitional function for himself or herself, but until one gains that skill, most contacts will likely be made through the mediation of subtle beings within the transitional realm.

I want to reiterate that this division into incarnate, transitional and higher-order realms is one way I have found convenient to model the subtle realms and their relationship to the physical world. It's based on personal encounters and experience. It helps me to orient myself and more or less predict what to expect from a particular encounter and how to prepare for it. But at the same time, it's very simplistic. It's like saying that everyone south of the Mason-Dixon Line in the United States speaks one way and everyone north of it speaks another way. It's easy to find examples where this is true, but it's also easy to find examples where it isn't. Furthermore, drawing a division between people with a southern accent and those without is not the only way to "map" the United States. Other maps and models are certainly possible. In the final analysis, the map that is most useful is the one you draw yourself based on your experience.

Where is the Sacred in all of this? Is it a higher-order realm in itself? I see it as the "string" on which all worlds are vibrating, that which makes the notes possible. I do not think of the Sacred as a subtle world as such. The Sacred is present in all things, all beings, all worlds, radiantly evident in some and densely hidden in others. In my own training, attuning to the Sacred is the foundation for all effective work with the non-physical worlds. Of course, what this means and how one may go about it depends on the individual and his or her particular spiritual tradition and practice.

There are traditions that recommend bypassing the subtle worlds altogether and focusing only on the Sacred or on Ultimate Beingness. I happened to comment to a friend of mine who is the Roshi of a Zen center that I had seen an angel overlighting the building that was being used as a meditation temple. He commented that in his tradition, such things were ignored as being distractions on the path to enlightenment. But he was interested in what I had seen and what I felt about such beings. I told him that for me such entities were simply a natural part of the universe, like trees and bears and people. I said that my contemplative, spiritual practice through which I sought attunement and oneness with sacredness was not the same as my work with the inner worlds. I did not look to an angel to grant me enlightenment but I did think of an angel as a potential partner in work for the world. This he could understand and accept.

There's a final thought I need to address in this overview. Hollywood, popular novels of horror and the supernatural, and some religious traditions would have you think that the subtle realms are inherently treacherous and that engaging with them is a dangerous thing to do. Frankly there *are* dangerous places and dangerous beings in the non-physical realms, particularly in what I call the transitional realms, as there can be in any large environment. It would be irresponsible to pretend otherwise. However, the danger can be—and usually is—greatly overblown.

I used to go hiking in the desert when I lived in Arizona. The desert certainly can be a dangerous place. One can die from heatstroke or dehydration, or from bites from poisonous reptiles, not to mention stumbling and falling in uneven terrain and being injured. I never went unprepared. I dressed appropriately, took plenty of water, wore suitable hiking boots, and kept an eye out for rattlesnakes, avoiding the places they were most likely to be. I was perfectly safe as long as I paid attention and exercised a reasonable degree of common sense, caution and desert savvy.

In sixty years of engaging with the subtle worlds, I have occasionally run into toxic places where the subtle energies were potentially harmful or at best unpleasant, but I have only twice run into anything close to a dangerous entity. I don't go into places where they might be found, and I don't do things to attract them. The subtle realms are not filled with predators just waiting to pounce upon and possess unwary people.

In this regard they are really no different from the physical world. If I were a policeman or a soldier on the battlefield, I would expect to enter into dangerous situations and meet dangerous individuals, but I'm not, so I don't. The subtle worlds have their dark alleys and places of conflict where dangerous conditions and beings may be found, but unless you seek them out or have some connection that draws you to them (usually anger, hatred and violence in your own heart); there is no reason for you to encounter them and plenty of reasons not to. And if you *do* feel yourself to be psychologically unstable or having mental and emotional difficulties, or if you are caught up in strong negative feelings such as hatred and anger, it's far better *not* to engage with the subtle worlds anyway until you have changed this and have greater stability and clarity. The best course in such a state is to seek out the Sacred where you may find healing, forgiveness, and transformation, in addition to any outer help you may find from people skilled in helping you find resolution and balance.

Engaging with subtle realms is not intrinsically dangerous. We are already part of these worlds anyway for our souls are higher-order beings. They are as much our home as the physical realm, and most of us engage with them on a daily basis while asleep as well as in other ways we may not be consciously aware of. But to engage with them consciously is a skill we can each develop, and the benefits to ourselves and to others can far outweigh the challenges. I hope my field notes will help you in this direction.

Field Notes Two: Why?

There is more to understanding the subtle worlds than simply having a cosmological model or an esoteric map of how they relate to each other or a listing of the kinds of beings one may encounter upon them. It is also important to understand what might be called, with no pun intended, the "spirit" behind the inner realms.

Perhaps a way to explore this is to ask why we want to engage with the subtle worlds in the first place, and why would they wish to engage with us. The answers may seem obvious, but we can learn a lot when we examine motivations.

People have sought out the inner beings for as long as human beings have walked the earth. The oldest known spiritual practice is shamanism which is a deliberate process for journeying into the non-physical worlds and seeking out subtle forces and subtle beings for cooperation, help, guidance, healing, instruction and the like. Shamanism is practiced in all manner of ways and uses a variety of methodologies, but in one form or another it is found all over the globe in nearly every culture that has existed. And if a culture bypasses the use of shamanic techniques, it still evolves some form of reaching out to the unseen worlds through prayer or ritual.

In other words, until approximately two hundred years ago with the development of modernity and the materialistic worldview, the existence of non-physical realms and beings was taken for granted. The conceptualization of those realms and beings varied from culture to culture and over time also as those cultures evolved and changed, but a general understanding has been fairly consistent. Some of the features usually agreed upon across time and culture have been the following: a place to which humans go when they die, a place of powerful spiritual forces such as angels, gods, and goddesses, a place of nature spirits associated with animals, plants and landscapes, and, often, a realm of darkness from which malevolent and evil forces emerge.

Because of this darker realm, non-physical beings have often been seen as uncaring and dangerous, given to trickery, deception, and illusion, if not outright evil. Such possibilities exist, just as they do in the physical world. But on the whole these beings and the realms they come from have generally been seen as sources of wisdom, spiritual Light, guidance, protection, healing, blessings, power, and other gifts that can bless and benefit physical life. Certainly in my experience such benign forces far and away predominate and define the essential nature of the inner worlds.

Because of this, an important reason that individuals have attempted throughout the ages to contact and engage with the subtle realms is in order to receive help of some nature. Another has been to associate with beings assumed to be spiritual in order to advance one's own spiritual development. Many years ago, I talked with a man who was studying to be a trance channel so he could contact inner beings and allow them to speak through him to others. When I asked him why he wanted to do that, he said, "In order to be spiritual." It was an answer I hadn't expected since I had never personally associated contact with subtle beings with spirituality or spiritual growth (and I still don't), but I have since found such an attitude not uncommon. In part, I feel, it's due to the confusion I already wrote about over the dual meaning of "spiritual." But it's also true that there are inner beings whose presence can be very inspirational and can encourage and nourish a deepening of our own spiritual natures.

The motives an individual may have for seeking engagement with the inner worlds are many, ranging from a variety of personal needs, to curiosity, to a desire to serve, and to be a more whole person. Understanding what your motive is for seeking engagement with subtle worlds is important, for a person's intent and desire can play a huge role both in determining what kind of contact is made and its subsequent integration and consequences in a person's life. Clarity of intent and accepting responsibility for that intent are important.

Also important is an awareness of possible weaknesses or biases that may affect the process. Are you given to self-aggrandizement? Do you have a need for recognition or to be thought of as special? Are you susceptible to drama and glamour? Are you vulnerable to self-deception? It may be hard to see such things in oneself, or hard to honestly admit them if we do suspect they're there, but such self-reflection and self-knowledge is vital. Personal weaknesses of this nature can become pitfalls later in the process. Here is where, as I describe in a later set of Field Notes, having a "buddy" who can give you honest reflection and feedback about yourself and your motives can be invaluable.

Of course, contact with subtle worlds can occur in a person's life without that person having sought or desired it. This is what happened to me. I have always been aware to some degree of a non-physical reality, and some of my earliest memories are of seeing and interacting with subtle beings who for the most part appeared to me simply as radiant figures of Light. I didn't seek this contact out anymore than I sought out seeing the sunlight or the flowers or hearing the people talking or the sound of music. They were all just part of my life and world, and I took them for granted growing up. I thought everyone was aware of non-physical beings and just didn't talk about it. Adults kept a lot of things secret, I felt when I was growing up, and I assumed this was just one of them. Consequently, I didn't talk about my experiences much either.

I didn't seek out my inner mentor John either when he showed up one day, but I had asked for help. Two weeks earlier I had left college in response to an inner calling I had been feeling for some months and was in Los Angeles trying my hand at giving talks on spirituality. I found myself being put in the role of a spiritual teacher, something for which I was not prepared, and I felt out of my depth. My background was in biology and organic chemistry; my original intent had been to become a molecular biologist working in the field of genetics. I had twenty years of experiencing non-physical beings, but I had no sense of what to do with those experiences or how to be a spiritual teacher even though I was inwardly convinced that this was what I was supposed to do. So I had prayed for help. And a couple days later, John appeared, offering me partnership, training, and friendship and basically saying that he had been waiting for me to come to a point in my life where we could work together as we had agreed to do before I was born.

So I had a dual motive of seeking help and guidance and of wanting to serve. As it turned out, John had motives, too. He had his own "why" for contacting me (quite apart from any pre-incarnational arrangements). In this he was not unusual. Working with him through the years, I discovered that many groups and beings within the unseen worlds had strong motivations for wishing to contact and work with incarnate people like us. However, for the most part, their motivations had one difference from those which many physical people bring to the effort to engage with the subtle worlds: they are not personal but are planetary in nature. They stem from a desire to serve the planet as a whole and all life upon it.

One of the main exceptions to this is found with human beings who have newly died and are in the early "Post-Mortem" or after-life realms, the transitional realms between the physical world and the higher-order worlds. Many people experience after death a natural desire to reconnect with their loved ones and friends, to let them know they're really still alive and OK. Even after some time has passed, they may still wish to help those they have left on earth, if only to mitigate the grief they may feel. And if the newly dead person has wronged people on earth, he or she may seek ways of making amends.

In short, there can be personal reasons for seeking contact with incarnate persons, and those reasons can lead someone to attempt to contact earthly individuals. It takes time for a person who is now dis-incarnate and learning to adjust to the vaster reality of the subtle worlds to begin to think beyond their individuality and into attunement with the larger wholes of which he or she is a part, thereby experiencing himself or herself as part of planetary life and beingness—unless, of course, this person has already been accustomed to thinking and attuning in this way while in a physical body. This does not mean the person "dissolves" into some collective consciousness; the core of individuality (which is different from the personality) is always retained. But it does mean that he or she gains a larger, more holistic perspective and experiences connectedness to the living spirit of the planet and the cosmos beyond. Attaining that connectedness and holistic consciousness, as well as training a person to live in a different reality of consciousness, is the function of the Post-Mortem Realms.

Those who live and function in the higher-order realms, on the other hand, deeply experience the wholeness and interconnectedness of life and act from that perspective. This does not mean that they always act skillfully, knowledgeably or with wisdom—higher-order beings can make mistakes, too, particularly in relationship to the very differently organized physical realm—but it does mean their motivation is to serve the whole, to create wholeness, and to advance the cause of life in all its forms.

In this they are expressing their own innate goodness, but they are also responding to the needs and intentions of the world soul, that life for whom the planet itself is its physical body. This being is not God, but it *is* a vast, highly evolved consciousness and presence whose work is to provide a complete and nourishing environment within which many kinds of life and sentiency may evolve. Honoring both ancient traditions and the modern scientific theory that the earth itself is a living entity, I call this being *Gaia*.

To really understand the subtle worlds, I have found it important to appreciate the existence and nature of this World Soul and to think of Gaia as a whole system. While we may identify divisions and separate elements within this system, it still functions as a wholeness in which every part is interconnected with every other part. This means that if humanity makes a mess of things "down here," the effects can be felt in the subtle world as well, particularly in the transitional realms which are generally "closer" to the physical plane energetically.

As much as anything, the problem is one of circulation. Just as I don't feel as fit and vital physically if I have clogged arteries and the flow of blood through my body is constricted, so the planet's potential vitality is lessened when the flow of subtle and sacred energies becomes obstructed. Humanity's general lack of wholeness and destructive behavior not only generates toxic subtle energies in the form of psychic pollution but it also can block and constrict the clear flow and circulation of vital subtle forces between ourselves and the subtle worlds. Powerful healing and nourishing subtle energies from the higher-order worlds can be denied entry into the incarnate realms or enter only partially or with distortion; likewise, vital subtle energies arising from the vitality and expression of the physical world into the transitional and higher-order worlds can be distorted or obstructed, too. Neither side may receive all the potential energizing nourishment that could be possible if such obstruction were not present.

Humanity has developed modern civilizations that are progressively and systematically damaging the planet, driving many forms of plant and animal life into extinction and even threatening ourselves with extinction. The potential effects of climate change and other environmental failures could lead to the deaths of millions, if not billions, of people. Death per se is not an issue for beings in the subtle worlds; if nothing else, they see and know that life is truly eternal and that the loss of a physical body does not mean the end of life or consciousness. On the other hand, when life is lost, and particularly if a species goes extinct, it's like slamming a door and shutting off part of the house, preventing anyone from using the rooms behind that door. Possibilities and potentials are lost, and complexity is reduced. Forms of incarnation that life might have used to engage with the material universe and become physical participants in the evolution of Gaia are no longer available. The overall circulation and manifestation of life, consciousness and energy throughout the whole planetary system is lessened. This diminishes all of us. And it affects the ability of the World Soul (or for that matter, that of the collective Soul of Humanity) to manifest all its potentials.

I have found through the years that the spirit of the World Soul permeates the subtle worlds of the earth, which is not surprising. I experience it as a presence of love, but I also experience it as a will that seeks wholeness and an expression of its capacity to realize its potentials. This is not surprising. I can feel in myself an urge to be a whole person and to have all my various elements—mind, emotion, body, spirit—working together in harmony and integration. Why should the spirit of the world be any different? This will manifests as a pressure towards greater integration and coherency, as well as towards creative freedom. The diminishment of life and consciousness on the physical level, whether through unnecessary extinctions or, in the case of humanity, through a loss of the freedom to express our creative and spiritual potentials, runs counter to this. Consequently, part of the will of the World Soul is to manifest conditions that will bring its scattered parts together in wholeness.

Consequently, many if not most of the beings I have encountered over the years embody and serve this planetary will as well as fulfilling their own particular and individual destinies and functions. For instance, when John came to me, he said that he was part of a group of beings whose work was to serve the World Soul in fostering the wholeness of the world. There are, of course, a great many ways in which this can be done, and in John's case, it was to help develop a spirituality that would support partnership, alliance, and collaboration between a human being and the inner worlds.

Over and over again, I have had subtle beings like John affirm that humanity could be so much more than it is and could live in a heaven on earth if we could heal the divisions that we have created between ourselves and each other, ourselves and nature, and ourselves and the subtle realms. Like the two hemispheres of the brain which each have specific functions and complement each other in producing a whole mind, so the incarnate worlds and the higher-order worlds, with the transitional realms serving a coordinating and blending function between them, each offer something important and necessary to each other and to the wholeness of the planet. Gaia is not complete with just one or the other. What is needed is a skillful, knowledgeable and loving collaboration between them.

Humanity is part of both worlds. We have physical bodies, minds and hearts which enable us to be part of and engage with the incarnate realms. But we also have subtle bodies and souls that are part of the transitional and higher-order worlds. When we are able to connect and synthesize these elements within us and find personal coherency and wholeness, we can be a bridge between these two halves of the planetary consciousness, able to synthesize and blend them in our own lives and behavior. This is the vision that John had—and that many inner beings have, for that matter—and is a reason he and his colleagues were motivated to do what they could to make such bridging and alliance possible.

Trying to make generalizations about the subtle worlds is risky. There are always exceptions to disprove almost any statement. The non-physical dimension as a whole is, after all, a vast, varied and dynamic interrelated set of environments expressing multiple states of consciousness. If I said that all Americans like apple pie and think baseball is the ultimate sport, I would be wrong. A number of my friends, for instance, prefer berry pies (and some don't like pies at all) and would much rather watch football. And some friends don't eat any desserts or watch any sports. So anything I say about the subtle worlds in a general way has to be taken lightly.

It would be incorrect, then, to say that all subtle beings are aligned with the World Soul or with this desire to foster its development, though all beings connected to the earth draw upon its life and presence to some degree. We find this same condition in our world where not everyone is knowledgeable or concerned about environmental issues or is trying to foster a more sustainable and holistic relationship between humanity and nature, even though all human beings draw upon nature for their sustenance. Many beings I have encountered, while good-natured and benign, are focused upon their specific area of responsibility and are not necessarily attuned to larger concerns. In this regard they are not unlike many people.

Nor is it true that all subtle beings seek to help out humanity or, in some cases, even have our best interests at heart. I have encountered beings on rare occasions who don't even know we exist or knowing it, have very little interest in humanity and its welfare, though they would not intentionally do anything to harm us.

Having said that, though, the general impression I have had over the past sixty years in dealing with these realms is one of a great and unconditional love and of a strong desire to help incarnate humanity move to a consciousness of wholeness. Consequently, I have found most beings on inner worlds by and large eager and desirous for humanity to succeed in its destiny and willing to help if they can.

What they can do to help depends on the kind of being they are, how close energetically they are to the physical plane, their own depth of understanding of our world, and training they may have had in "interdimensional" work. And no matter how trained, willing, or able they may be, there are still important restrictions which might be summed up by saying they can't do anything we can or should do for ourselves. (There are beings in the transitional realms who may try to violate this because they have a love of their own power and enjoy manipulating humans or they have a need to be needed or seen as teachers and guides; if any subtle being offers to take over and do things for me or is too free and insistent with guidance, my standard reply is "Thanks, but no thanks. Just be on your way!")

Many people, influenced no doubt by fictional accounts of the powers of subtle beings, assume they can do anything they wish, and if they want to help us, can do so. This is far from the truth. The differences between the physical world and the non-physical worlds are considerable, and subtle beings are not all-powerful, whatever horror writers would like us to believe in order to tell an exciting story. Just for a start, they don't have bodies. It's very hard to influence physical matter without a body! Not that it can't be done, but there is an energy cost to the process, and most subtle beings do not have the energy resources or capacities to pay that cost.

Other factors enter in as well. All things being equal, if a physical person has a strong intention to do something and is using his or her will to see that it's done, he or she will exert a much more powerful influence within the physical world than a comparable non-physical being trying to will this person to stop and not do that thing. The physical person is in resonance with physical activity and energy, whereas the subtle being is not.

This doesn't mean the subtle being is helpless. If it has the knowledge, the skill, and the energy to do so, it can attempt to influence the fields of subtle energy within a particular physical environment to influence probabilities, and it can also attempt to communicate to the subconscious of the individual, if not directly to his or her conscious mind and emotions. But how often do we listen to the still, small voice of conscience within us rising from our subconscious mind when we are bound and determined to have our way with something?

Even more important than the sheer capacity (or lack of it) for intervention, there are principles of action and consequence—some might say principles of karma—and of free will that cannot be abridged or overridden. This is particularly true of higher-order beings who will not deliberately weaken a person by interfering with his or her free will or with the learning of lessons, even hard ones. The basic principle is that if we mess it up, we need to fix it; if we are responsible, we need to deal with the consequences. Of course, we can get help, but inner beings can't do it all for us. They can, however, be our partners.

Over the years I have observed four major ways that subtle beings can and do help us. One is by intervening to handle anything we can't handle ourselves yet. This particularly is true about cleansing, transforming, or otherwise getting rid of toxic subtle energies that we generate with our negativity or violence. They can't get rid of all of it; only we can do that. But they can keep the psychic pollution from becoming too overwhelming. This is not entirely altruistic on their part, for particularly in the transitional realms, they may have to work in the subtle realms that we pollute, so they may have to take action in order to keep the energies they require or work with circulating. But some of that pollution is caught within the fields of human thought and feeling where essentially it is out of reach or out of bounds for them, unless we partner with them to clear it away in shared acts of subtle energy hygiene. In other words, we have to let go of negative psychic conditions to which we may be attached and provide our own will and energy to allow transformation and cleansing to take place.

It has been my observation that however bad the world seems to be to us, it would be a good deal worse were it not for this kind of benign intervention.

A second way is by seeding the realms of thought and feeling with ideas and qualities that human beings can pick up on and be inspired by. We, of course, will usually experience these things as if they originated within us. These can include ideas for inventions, techniques, processes, stories, institutions, scientific breakthroughs, new forms of politics and economics, and so forth.

It is *not* true, as some have suggested, that all good, transformative, and helpful ideas come from the non-physical dimensions with human minds simply acting as receivers. Our minds and hearts are sacred instruments, and we are quite capable of generating insights and innovations on our own. We are each creative individuals as much as any inner being may be. But this doesn't mean that subtle beings cannot also contribute collaboratively to a general pool of knowledge and insight. Furthermore, our own creativity is often constricted by our fears and feelings of limitation. We have been told in so many ways by so many sources that as human beings we are flawed, limited, incapable, negative, and even at times evil that we behave as if this were so. We have our problems and are not perfect by any means, but we also have great resources of spirit, intellect, love and creativity within us. All the subtle beings I've ever worked with fully acknowledge this and yearn for the time when we can stand in our beauty and power as their partners in sacredness and co-creative collaboration.

A third way subtle beings help is by directly offering guidance and instruction to those who can receive it. This can happen in a myriad of ways other than direct communication. For instance, it can happen through dreams. Care needs to be taken with this approach on both sides. The inner being needs to be careful not to abrogate the incarnate individual's free will, even unintentionally. The incarnate human, on the other hand, needs to exercise discernment and discrimination. Unfortunately, as I said earlier, there are subtle beings, particularly in the lower transitional realms, that are essentially meddling busybodies who love to be seen as sources of guidance and direction. I'll discuss this more fully in a later set of Field Notes.

More problematic, perhaps, is that higher-order beings can be loving and wise but not always earth-smart. They may be well-intentioned but have either forgotten or never knew or understood conditions in the incarnate realms. Their advice may sound good in theory and principle but not work well in practice or may even cause harm. A human being should never abandon his or her own good judgment, common sense or principles in the face of guidance.

Indeed, the very first week John and I began working together he gave me this piece of advice: "Always feel free to say 'No' to me or to any inner being no matter how exalted it may seem. The ability to say no is as important to your freedom and sovereignty as the power to say yes, and your freedom and sovereignty are vital to the work we're to do. Without the right and ability to say no to each other, we cannot have a free and creative partnership."

The fourth mode of helping is energetic in nature and consists of a blending of the presence and energies of the subtle being with those of the incarnate human being in a manner that creates a larger and more potent field than either could manage on his or her own. This is the principle behind the saying that if you take God's hand in yours and walk together, you can accomplish miracles. Such collaborative fields can manifest qualities that emerge when the different elements of the planet come together in wholeness. They can be like Gaia in miniature.

On the mental level, such a field results in the creation of what I call *collaborative mind*. This is actually a familiar concept and experience. It's a principle used often in human relationships when we sit around and brainstorm or share ideas together in collaborative ways. At such times, we can feel the field of shared thought that we are co-creating and which is inspiring and empowering our individual thinking. Subtle beings are very good at this, I've found, and it was a major way that John and I worked together. It expresses the essence of good partnership.

In all four of these cases, an underlying principle is that doors open and opportunities arise for collaboration when we ask. I have found over and over again in my work with subtle beings that they may have riches to offer, but often I have to ask before they can deliver them. This asking is not in a needy way but is a respectful and loving invitation to be part of my world.

I would sum up my overall impression of the subtle worlds in this way. They and the physical realm are both part of a single, whole planetary system. To further the wholeness and wellbeing of this system, they seek to build with us collaborative and loving partnerships. We can participate in such partnerships when we engage with them with clarity, freedom, and the sovereignty of our individual uniqueness and sacredness. Such partnerships embody the spirit of service and a dedication to the highest good of all concerned.

Field Notes Three:
How?

At this point, you, Dear Reader, may well be thinking that it's all well and good to talk about the importance of partnering with the subtle worlds and the benefits that may come from this, but how does one go about it? Now that I've given some overviews of the terrain and some general impressions of the non-physical realms, what can I say about methodology? How do I engage with non-physical beings and the realms from which they come? How does anyone?

To understand the process, we must first appreciate that human beings have multiple levels of consciousness. If I go back to the analogy of the subtle worlds being like notes existing along a guitar string, then a human being is a chord of those notes. There is a part of each of us that exists in the higher-order worlds (I call that part the *soul*), in the transitional realms (I call that part our *incarnate soul* or *high self*), and in the subtle energy fields of the incarnate realms (this part is made up of our *subtle bodies*). Of course, these are in addition to our physical bodies. Each of these aspects of ourselves connects us more or less to its corresponding realm, just as our physical bodies connect us to the material world around us.

Our physical body has organs of perception that connect us to the world around us; this is equally true of the other levels of our being. In fact, it is probably more accurate to say that the whole of ourselves extending from the soul to the body is an "organ" of perception, of which specific senses, such as—on the physical level— sight and hearing, are particular manifestations. We are embodied awareness at every level.

This awareness expresses itself physically through our familiar senses of sight, hearing, smell, taste, and touch. When we consider our non-physical nature, as one goes "up the levels" from the subtle dimension of the incarnate realms through the transitional realms into the higher-order worlds and the domain of the soul, our innate awareness expresses as subtle perception (clairvoyance, for instance, or extra-sensory perception), imagination, intuition, inspiration, and something I call *imbuement.* In each case, the nature of perception becomes less and less dichotomous and objective (that is, see an outside world separate from ourselves and experiencing a separation between subject and object) and more participatory. With imbuement, a person doesn't perceive so much as he or she becomes. I have experienced this often in dealing with higher-order beings: we become one and I experience the object of perception from the inside-out, so to speak, as if I were that which I perceive. Any sense of separation between me as subject and the object of perception dissolves. I am "imbued" with the nature and essence of what I perceive or of the being with whom I am communicating. This was the predominant manner in which John and I communicated.

In this latter process, it was important that I retain a sense of identity even in the midst of a profound merging with John or another being. The object was not to become one *per se* but to communicate, in this case through a process of deep communion. Part of my training was in how to do this, and it relied upon developing and strengthening an inner quality I call *sovereignty.*

In my experience, training in subtle perception consists of two processes. One is to energize awareness at a particular level or with a particular form of inner perception—in effect opening or widening the processes of perception at that level of energy and consciousness. The other is to build the connections between these levels within oneself so that the different parts of ourselves can communicate more freely and fully together in integrated and harmonious ways. This is particularly true of opening connections with our brain-mind, which is the level of consciousness most of us use every day and which is designed to connect with the physical world, not with non-physical dimensions. In one way, we are all practicing and experiencing subtle awareness all the time; information from all levels is coming to us from the totality of our being. But just as we are only partially aware of all the data our physical senses pick up from the environment and relay to the brain, so we are usually only partially aware, if aware at all, of information coming from non-physical senses.

There are natural filters and boundaries that exist between the physical, conscious mind and the non-physical levels of perception and information. They are there for good reasons to prevent us from being swamped with information that we cannot interpret or integrate. I believe these filters or "veils" withdraw naturally as a person becomes ready to deal with an increased level of stimulation. Trying to force them open ahead of time, particularly through drugs, is asking for trouble. So a large part of the training to gain subtle awareness consists of building proper foundations of psychological and energetic balance within oneself and developing means of integrating the enhanced energies that come with awakening inner perceptions.

In my own case as a child, I had an awareness of the subtle energy fields of the incarnate realms and occasionally of beings who would enter and appear within such fields. I believe that many children, if not most of them, have this experience to some degree, especially as infants. When I was seven, however, I had an out-of-body experience that awakened me to my soul, that is, to the part of me that is normally conscious and aware within the higher-order worlds. This was like seeing into two worlds simultaneously, the world of the soul and the world of the body.

As a child, I did not know what to do with this awareness, so it withdrew somewhat. I was always aware that it was there but in the background. However, it was this awareness that was heightened by my studies in math and science in college, and by the time I was nineteen, it had come to the forefront of my awareness. This is what prompted me to leave school and become a spiritual teacher. When John came into my life soon after, the training he offered me was to help me engage with that higher-order level of consciousness and to integrate it more strongly into my conscious, everyday awareness. He gave me the tools I needed to engage with it so that I could, in effect, perceive and think with two different minds at once.

However, I have never been very effective in attuning to or

perceiving within the transitional realms, which is where a great deal of what people normally think of as clairvoyant perception takes place. I am aware of the subtle energy fields around me within the incarnate world and of the higher-order worlds (some of them, anyway), but not of much in-between. In fact, once as a teenager I had a friend who was a trained clairvoyant who was very good at seeing into the transitional realms. He offered to teach me how to do so as well and gave me some exercises to practice. However, when I started to practice them, a higher-order being appeared and asked me to stop. "If you develop this mode of perception," he said, "it will block or interfere with the perceptions you already have." It would, I realized later, have created a barrier between my physical mind and the higher-order worlds to which I was attuned. So I stopped the exercises and never pursued them again.

This story leads me to an important point. All inner development is personal and unique. It's an organic process rooted in the distinctness and differences of a person's incarnation. There are shared principles, but especially when it comes to subtle awareness and engaging non-physical worlds, the process is different for each person. This is because we're really talking about creating relationships. The subtle worlds are far more participatory and subjective than anything we're used to in the physical world, so the particularity and specificity of your unique nature are important ingredients in the process.

A cursory perusal of the Internet will uncover many resources for developing psychic abilities, clairvoyance, and the like. There certainly are many different kinds of techniques available for doing so. But many if not most of them treat subtle perception as if it were simply another form of physical perception and the subtle organs of perception (such as the fabled "third eye" of clairvoyance) as if they were analogues of our physical senses. In my experience, the more we engage with the subtle worlds and develop the means to do so, the more we realize that we don't perceive with some subtle organ of perception but with our whole beings. As I said earlier, our whole incarnation from body to soul is the "organ of perception." When we understand this, then we realize that the core of any training in subtle awareness is really a training in integrating the various levels and elements of one's life and developing coherency and wholeness between them.

For this reason, in my own classes, the process of training begins not with subtle perception per se but with understanding and integrating oneself and with the development of the quality I call *sovereignty*. As it was for me working with John, the training I offer must be grounded in the wholeness of one's incarnation and its connectedness to the world. This is particularly important because as our awareness moves beyond the subtle dimensions of the incarnate realms and into the transitional realms and the higher-order worlds beyond, communication becomes less and less information-oriented and more and more a process of exchanging and sharing life, energy and presence. Being able to participate in this kind of exchange without being overwhelmed and suffering incoherency in the process is the necessary foundation at the heart of subtle awareness.

My own training with John was more in the form of an apprenticeship. Lessons were intimately integrated with what was going on in my life. In this process, I learned in ways I might not have known otherwise how individualized contact with the subtle worlds is and how much it is rooted in the organic wholeness of our lives.

We have physical analogues for this. For instance, while the process of tasting is the same for all of us, the experience of tasting is not. For my wife, licorice is sweet. For me it is bitter. My father had an extremely sensitive sense of taste that made him a fabulous cook, which was his hobby. He could taste something someone had cooked and tell you exactly what ingredients were in it and often their proportions. I have nowhere near that discriminating a palate. Dad could rhapsodize over the subtle flavors in a meal at a French restaurant; for me, though, the food was bland and left me wishing for a bottle of ketchup. Anyone training Dad and me in cooking would have to take these differences in our tasting abilities into account. Just handing us each a recipe and telling us to follow the directions would not give the best results. Individual attention would be the best approach.

Furthermore, John did not train me as a student. He worked

with me as a partner and collaborator, in effect enabling me to train myself. I was directing the process as much as he was, though in different ways.

Although I can't train a person in the way John trained me, for the simple reason that I'm not a non-physical being and thus lack some of the capacities John had, I can follow his principles. And one of them is to respect the individuality of the person I'm working with. For this reason, I don't attempt to give lessons in how to develop subtle perception or engage with the non-physical worlds in this book. I don't know who you are. Training for me needs to be interactive and collaborative. My job would be to help you train yourself. Because your life is individual and unique, there's no one "right" way to do that. The way needs to unfold.

But there are some basic, common principles. One of these is that every engagement with the subtle worlds that we initiate has three parts. I'll call them Pre-Contact, Contact, and Post-Contact.

By Pre-Contact I mean the things that a person routinely does to build an ongoing foundation for contact and engagement with subtle worlds. One of these is to lead as broad and rich a life as possible and appropriate. John encouraged me to have hobbies, to study a wide variety of subjects, and to have a broad range of contacts and friends. Keeping the mind supple and always open and learning was important.

Equally important was having a solid ethical and moral practice, one based on love, compassion and harmlessness more than on legalistic prescriptions of do's and don'ts. Maintaining one's integrity is an important part of the development and maintenance of the quality I call sovereignty. Sovereignty as I use the term is partly the capacity to be self-governing, to make one's own decisions and choices and to accept responsibility for them. It is also the capacity to hold a center within oneself and create integration and coherency between the various parts of one's being. Sovereignty honors one's boundaries, preventing them from becoming too rigid or too permeable. Sovereignty maintains the core of "I-ness"—the sacred essence of one's being—in the midst of the dynamic and fluid processes of incarnation and engagement with the world. Behavior that is unethical and damages or infringes upon the sovereignty of another damages one's own sovereignty as well, creating weakness and vulnerability when it comes to holding subtle energies, particularly from the higher-order worlds.

People sometimes have an image of ethical behavior as being narrow, dour, and judgmental. But in fact it's joyous, spacious, and life-affirming, the product of an open and loving heart embracing all the world as kin.

When I began working and studying with John, he gave me four practices to follow as a foundation for my training. These were attunement to self, attunement to sacredness, attunement to the subtle environment in the physical world around me, and blessing.

By attunement to self, John meant doing those things that honored my personality and the incarnational processes that linked it with my soul. From these processes a spiritual energy is generated in each of us that I call our incarnational Light or our Self-Light. This Light is innate in us, a product of the act of incarnation itself and our engagement with the energies of the earth and the World Soul. Our activities in life, our behavior, and the way we think and feel about ourselves can nourish and brighten it or can smother and diminish it. This Self-Light is an important resource in engaging with and gracefully holding the Light and the subtle, spiritual energies that come from the inner worlds, particularly from higher-order beings (including from our own souls). Attending to the nourishment and enhancement of this Self-Light is what John meant by "attuning to self," in addition to the other advice he gave about study, broadening the scope of one's life, and having activities that bring joy, recreation, and fulfillment to us.

Attunement to sacredness only partly meant attunement to the Sacred. John fully acknowledged the existence and power of the Sacred but never attempted to define it, saying that was mine to do for myself. However, by "sacredness" he meant those activities that bring love, compassion, joy and empowerment into the world. Part of my training consisted of exercises in loving, forgiveness, kindness, and compassion.

By attunement to sacredness, John also meant having a practice that took me beyond myself and my self-concerns and attuned me to a larger, more spacious consciousness and reality. If attunement to self focused on the particular and the individual, then attunement to sacredness expanded that to open to the universal. This is the incarnational balance we all seek to achieve: honoring and developing our unique individuality with its particular gifts and talents while also honoring and developing our connections with others and the service we can do on behalf of the world.

The physical environment in which we live also has a subtle, energy counterpart to which the subtle energy fields of everyone and everything in that environment contribute. As part of my training, John wished me to practice attuning to this subtle environment. In a way, I had been doing this since childhood, for I had been aware of this level of reality—the subtle dimension of the incarnate realms, sometimes called the etheric realm in esoteric literature—for as long as I could remember. But I had also taken it for granted and had not paid it too much attention unless something about it caught my notice. John wanted me to pay attention to it.

This level of awareness is one that most of us have and employ daily, though we may not think of it as such. It often takes the form of a felt sense, something we feel in our bodies. We may sense an "atmosphere" or mood in a room or in a place in nature; it might feel comforting and pleasant, or it might feel unpleasant, distressing or even dangerous. Or we sense such an atmosphere around a person. Such a sensing may take the form of a "gut feeling" or a hunch.

For example, a friend of mine told me of being hired to move some furniture to an old house. He did this, but as he was standing in the house, he felt such a sense of danger and unpleasantness that he turned and rushed outside, not even waiting for the full payment he had been promised. "I felt like it could be worth my life to stay in there," he said. On a more positive note, another friend of mine was promoted in his job and given an office on one of the upper floors of the skyscraper where he worked. He immediately set about blessing this room and putting things in it that he felt had good spiritual energies around them. He had no sooner settled in than other office workers began dropping by just to spend time in his room. Often they had no real excuse to be there and had actually come up the elevator from two or three levels below. One man said, "I'm not sure why, but I just felt I wanted to pop in and see you. It feels so good in here!"

This kind of awareness usually happens at a subconscious level for most people, but by paying attention to our feelings and sensings, we can elevate such awareness into a more conscious and deliberate state. This was what John wished me to do in order to develop greater perception of the subtle energies that are always around us, a simple first step to the deeper kinds of perception one needs in engaging with the transitional and higher-order worlds.

The final practice is that of blessing. This can mean the actual act of invoking or giving blessings to others or to the world around you, but it also means any activity that is kind, helpful, loving, compassionate, and enhancing of another. If the other three were basically inner practices, this one is outward-directed and active. I think of it as having a practice each day to make my world—the world I can see, touch, and influence—better than it was, or at the very least, no worse than it was. Of course, this can take many forms depending on circumstances, where you are, what you're doing, and so forth, but as a practice, it means being open to opportunities to be a presence and a force for blessing.

These four practices are at the center of pre-contact development and preparation. They can create a strong and radiant foundation of Self-Light and sovereignty for any engagement with the subtle worlds.

In addition, there is a final form of preparation and development. This is the training of the imagination.

It's been easy in our hard-headed, pragmatic, materialistic culture to dismiss the imagination as being a doorway leading away from the real world into fantasy, having little value except to creative artists. But show me a scientist who cannot use the powers of imagination, and I'll show you a mediocre technician. Show me a practical businessman who does not use imagination, and I'll show you either a failure or someone who is always playing catch-up to more successful rivals. Imagination is a powerful tool of perception, particularly in letting us see what could be as well as what is. It is the portal to potential and possibility. Everything we enjoy as the fruits of human invention and innovation began as a gleam of imagination. When we plan for the future, we are using our imaginations. Without imagination, we literally cannot picture tomorrow—or at least not a tomorrow that is any different from today or yesterday.

But in the context of engaging and working with subtle worlds, I'm thinking not so much of imagination as a power of vision and creativity or as a means for storytelling or fantasy, but as a tool of cognition. Think of a mathematical equation, like $E = mc^2$. As Einstein showed, this arrangement of letters, symbols, and a number has the power to transform the world. From it came the atomic bomb and nuclear energy. But what is the process by which this equation has meaning in our minds? What images arise in the mind of a mathematician or physicist who sees it? How does one think into and understand an equation like this—or any equation?

For that matter, what power of mind allows us to decipher letters and words on a page? We usually don't think in words as much as we think in images and concepts which we then use words to describe. But how often have you had the experience of knowing what you want to say but not finding the words to say it? This may not be a problem of insufficient vocabulary. It may be that the concepts in your mind have more depth or texture or qualities than mere words can quite capture or convey.

When you see the word "tree," you don't simply see four letters on a page. In your mind this word expands to become images of leafy organisms with trunks and roots. You may think of a particular tree or you may think of many trees, a forest of trees. In addition, you may think of all the uses to which a tree may be put, from bearing fruits to providing lumber.

There are vast concepts in the universe that are not easily described in words but which can be represented by symbols, equations, and the like. $E = mc^2$ is a simple arrangement of characters, but the ideas it represents and all their possibilities are complex. Whole books have been written based on this equation alone and the concepts associated with it.

I think of the power to unpack meaning from a word or from an equation like $E = mc^2$ (not to mention to write it in the first place) as conceptual or cognitive imagination. It's like the program on my computer that "unzips" and expands a compressed file so that I have access to it and can read it. This kind of imagination takes a symbol and extracts an often complex bundle of meaning and images from it. It is not trying to conceive of new forms in the way an artist might imagine a new painting or a new novel. I think of this kind of imagination as meaning-oriented rather than form-oriented. It translates words and images into concepts and meaning. It enlarges and expands.

It is this kind of imagination that I have found indispensible in working with the subtle worlds, particularly with beings from the higher-order realms. In the majority of cases in communicating with these beings, they do not use words and sometimes not even images (in the sense of narrative pictures that tell a story and thus communicate a meaning); they communicate in symbols and blocks of compressed energy and meaning. My friend the poet and cultural historian William Irwin Thompson calls this "hieroglyphic communication," and it's a good term for it. I can't use my logical mind to reason out meaning from such communications. I have to "unpack" them imaginatively.

I developed this imagination in the first place through my studies in science and mathematics when I was in college working to become a molecular biologist. In fact, this is what precipitated the change that took me out of college led me to become a spiritual teacher. As I developed my conceptual imagination through the study and use of abstract concepts and equations, I found that my communication with higher-order beings began to improve, which led to an increased level of contact. Eventually, I realized that this was the direction I needed to go in, rather than into the laboratory. Truth to tell, while I was very good with scientific concepts, I was a klutz in the lab, so my decision to become a spiritual teacher probably saved the scientific world from some disastrous laboratory accident.

This kind of imagination can be developed in different ways. Science and math worked for me, but poetry can have a similar effect. The art of poetry is to compress many layers of meaning into a very few words carefully and skillfully chosen. Unpacking those layers—and even discovering new ones the poet might not have realized were there—is part of the pleasure of reading poetry, but it can also be a powerful form of training in developing the kind of conceptual (or I could even say "poetic") imagination so useful for communication with subtle world beings.

One practice that I evolved was using tarot cards to help with this development. I have a large collection of tarot or tarot-like decks which I use not for divination or oracular purposes but just to explore the images and let them work in my imagination. The question I bring to such a practice is not "what does this card mean?" and not even "What story does this card tell?" Instead, I ask "What is evoked in me energetically and imaginatively as I look at the images and symbols in this card. What comes alive in me spiritually?" I keep my mind as open as possible, avoiding preconceptions and expectations.

I find this useful because as I said earlier, one of the modes of perception and communication with higher-order worlds is through something I call "imbuement." In effect, I am imbued with "meaningful energy" or a "meaningful presence." I become something other than what I was energetically, and this change of conceptual or inner shape conveys meaning. This meaning comes alive in me as a felt sense, as imagery, as presence, all of which acts like an equation in my mind, something for me to unpack with the conceptual imagination. I pay attention, in other words, to what is evoked in me in a full-bodied way.

Even this is hard to describe in words. Drawing on my former studies in cell biology, what I am reminded of is how a cell communicates with its environment. Protein molecules possessing a certain molecular shape extend through the cell wall into the surrounding environment. Part of this molecule is inside the cell in touch with other protein molecules in the cytoplasm or body of the cell and part of it is outside, poking out through the cell membrane. When it encounters something to which it is sensitive, this molecule responds by changing its shape. This shape change then triggers those molecules in the cytoplasm with which it is in touch to change their molecular shape as well. Since each shape carries or represents specific information, the cascading sequence of shape changes conveys information into the interior of the cell, which can then use that information to respond.

But this is just a metaphor when speaking of communication with higher-order beings. I use it because John used the concept of shape and shape change frequently in his training and communication with me. "Every thought and emotion has an energetic shape," he would say. He would then ask me to feel into a specific thought (like, say, "freedom" or "love") or a specific emotion (such as "fear" or "serenity" or "happiness") and sense what the shape of that thought or feeling was. He would ask, "If you were that emotion or thought, what would you look like energetically?" There was no right answer to such a question, only a practice of attuning to my subtle energy field (which was one of the four practices anyway) to get a sense of the pattern or configuration it was taking on when I was holding certain mental or emotional energies. This configuration was the energetic shape, and it was associated with a set of meanings. That is, it carried information.

Later, when I would be in contact with a higher-order being (beings I met in the transitional realms did not do this as much), I could feel my energetic shape changing, and if that being imbued me with its presence, energy and meaning, that shape change could be pronounced. And that change carried the essence of the communication. I became the communication rather than just receiving it from outside myself like we hear someone speaking to us. It was that new shape, that communication, that meaning that I had to unpack for my everyday mind to grasp it, and for that I needed to use my conceptual (or poetic) imagination.

This is why imagination is important. Anything you do that stimulates and heightens your powers of imagination, whether it's of the creative or the conceptual variety, will help you in engaging with subtle worlds.

Broadening and deepening the content of your life, having and following an ethical core to your activities and behavior, following the four practices, and developing your imagination are all part of laying the foundation in your life for engaging the subtle worlds. They are part of what I think of as the "pre-contact" preparation. But what about contact itself? How does one go about that?

Again, there are many ways contact can be made (and I'm assuming here that you are the one initiating the contact and not the other way around). The process, as I've said, is very individual. And one approach may work at one time for you while a different approach may be needed another time, depending on your own state of mind and heart at the time, the environment in which you find yourself, and the nature of the subtle beings or forces which you wish to contact. I cannot pretend to know just what may be needed or the particular training you may have already received.

But generally speaking, here is one way that I go about it, and you can see what in this process seems useful to you.

I want to be perfectly clear that there is no unconsciousness involved. I do not go into any kind of trance, nor do I recommend that approach. We want to bring to bear upon the contact with the subtle worlds the full weight of our intellectual, emotional, energetic, and spiritual capacities and resources. We come as partners and collaborators, not as instruments or "tubes" for them to speak through.

In taking this approach, which was also the only approach that John would condone in his work with me, I am fully aware that I can make mistakes and that even with the best will in the world, I may bring unwanted biases and preconceptions to the process. I have to take responsibility for who and what I am and what I bring to the partnership and for the consequences of it afterwards. An adult, co-creative partnership simply isn't possible unless I do so.

Once in my work with John, I was feeling the weight of this responsibility and the chance—even the likelihood, given human fallibility—that I might make mistakes. I broached the possibility of doing the work in a trance state in which I would go to sleep and he would simply speak through me. He laughed and said, "We'd rather you make mistakes than be unconscious. Mistakes we can correct. There's nothing we can do with unconsciousness."

In short, engagement with the subtle worlds is a mindful

process, an exercise in awareness.

My preparation in the moment is simply to stand in my sovereignty as a person and enter into a calm state of mind. I know that I will need to hold in myself whatever energies come from and with the contact I wish to make. When working with higher-order beings in particular but to some extent with any subtle being, different energetic effects are possible. I may simply feel more energized and stimulated as the energy field of the contact touches or merges with my own. There is every possibility that I may feel ecstatic and deeply loved, something I experience often with higher-order beings. Alternatively, if the contact is very different from me, perhaps non-human in its origin such as a nature being or a being that doesn't normally interact with incarnate human beings, I can experience the difference in negative ways, just as I might when meeting a physical person who is very different from me.

I remember once walking towards the door of a store I wished to enter and seeing coming from the opposite direction down the street towards the same store a young man and woman dressed in Goth style all in black. The young man had spiky black hair and piercings in his nose, lips, eyebrows, and ears. Chains were attached to his belt and looped down low around his thighs. His black jeans were torn at the knees. He looked ferocious and scary, and his female companion wasn't any gentler in her make-up and appearance. Seeing that we were going to arrive at the door of the store at the same time, I felt a momentary panic. As they say in the vernacular, their appearance "rattled" my mental and emotional cages, and I thought maybe I should turn and go in a different direction to avoid any meeting or possible confrontation. But the only threat was in my own imagination, and I didn't want to give in to such negative images or be rude in my response to them.

We arrived at the door at the same time, and to my surprise, the young man stepped forward, opened the door for me and in the sweetest and most polite manner, he said, "After you, sir." I was surprised and delighted, and immediately began laughing inwardly at my own concerns. I had been giving too much weight to a stereotype which, as it turned out, had no relationship to the reality. It was a good lesson for me.

In a similar manner, some subtle beings who are very different from human beings can carry energies that initially feel frightening or disturbing because of that difference but who in fact are loving and compassionate entities. So I need to be ready to hold whatever energy comes my way and not react until I have a chance to more deeply attune to the nature of the contact.

The hardest energies to handle in this manner, I've found, are not the ones that initially seem disturbing but the ones that fill me with ecstasy. To be filled with great joy and yet stand calm in that presence so the link isn't broken when what I really feel like doing is racing about with a smile on my face and dancing for that joy can be a real challenge.

I also begin by attuning widely to what is in my environment, acknowledging and making loving connections to the things around me, the furniture, the floor, the walls, the ceiling, (or if I'm outdoors, to the land, the grass, the trees, the birds, the animals that may be nearby). All these things are my energetic allies. By attuning to them I accomplish three things. I put myself in a larger incarnational context, I honor my physical status by honoring and connecting to my physical environment, and I gain allies in holding the subtle energies that may come through the contact. By building these links, I can distribute these subtle forces out into my immediate environment and not have to hold them all myself.

Using a physical analogy, making contact with and holding the impact of a high-energy higher-order being can be like trying to catch a 500-pound person leaping from a rooftop. If I try to do so on my own, I will in all likelihood be squashed. But if I have a fireman's net which is held not only by me but by many others as well, the kinetic energy of the falling man is distributed by that net more widely so no one takes the full brunt of it when he is caught.

Finally, I make sure I am attuned to my body and the felt sense that it can offer. This is important. Our bodies are very ancient and have a deep intelligence. They can sense things that our conscious minds may miss or misinterpret. If there is anything wrong, misleading, or dangerous about the energy and presence of a subtle being, your body will most likely react negatively to it, whereas your mind and heart may be taken in by the glamour or the words of that entity. If your body feels restless or has a negative response to a contact, I suggest paying attention to it. It isn't always right, but the body intelligence is often more and better aware on a subtle level than the conscious mind is. This is all the more reason not to go into a trance where awareness of body states and felt senses are cut off.

When I was six years old, I decided I could tightrope walk across a high wire running from the wall of our house to a pole across the yard. My mother hung clothes from this wire normally, but I thought it looked like an invitation to adventure. Needless to say, I fell off and landed on some boards, hurting my back. No permanent damage was done (I was lucky!) but I have always had a weakness there. Interestingly, in working with John or with other subtle beings, if I am misinterpreting something or getting a communication wrong, that part of my back will begin to ache. Over the years, I've learned this is a fairly reliable body signal that something is not right and that I should stop and reevaluate. In this and other ways, when it comes to working with the inner worlds, I have found my body to be one of my best allies.

I wrote in the last Field Notes about the loving and intentional impulse from the subtle worlds to create wholeness between their realms and ours. I call this a *holopoietic* impulse, that is, a desire and urge to create wholeness, integration and coherency. In reaching out to the subtle worlds, I want to find that same impulse in me and stand in it. In other words, I want to be in empathy and resonance with the kind of energies and intentions to which I wish to attune.

This is just good sense. If you come to me and say you want to work with me, I will be more open to the proposition and more likely to connect with you if you are in harmony with what I'm trying to do. The higher-order beings in particular come with a love for the world and an intent to bless it; you will have an easier time attuning to them if you share this love, not just conceptually but as a real passion within your own heart.

At this point, the actual mechanism of contact consists of shifting my attention inward and outward, shifting my awareness to the existence and nature of subtle energies. If there is a particular kind of being I wish to contact whose characteristics I know, then I hold those characteristics in my mind. I form an energetic image—that is, an image of the qualities and character—of that being in my imagination and reach out to that image requesting contact. I may call upon other non-physical allies to help me. And then I just wait to see what happens. It's quite possible that no contact will ensue, but usually it will.

As in any endeavor, experience counts for a great deal here. Obviously when you're starting out, you lack that experience. So you go slowly, pay attention, and learn from every experience. In time you will build up an "energy rolodex," a sense of what various kinds of contacts feel like energetically, which gives you the clues on how to connect with them. Initially, though, you may need to imagine what such a contact might be like. If, for instance, you seek contact with a healing angel but have no idea what one feels like, imagine what such a being might be like, not in appearance or form but in its energy and qualities. What do you think you would feel like in the presence of such a being? Imagine your own state of mind or your bodily felt sense in such a situation. Use that imagination as a point of focus and bring your attention to it. Hold it within you. What attracts and connects is your intention as much as anything.

Once contact has been completed, you enter the Post-Contact phase which is just as important as the other two. I devote one of my later Field Notes to it. Essentially this is the time for discernment, integration of whatever effects or energies have resulted from the contact, planning your next steps, and so forth. It is the step of completion and resolution of the particular contact.

To complete these Field Notes, let me reiterate that there is no one "right way" to contact and communicate with inner beings. There are important principles, but the actual process is an individual one. For this reason, I think of the process of training to do this as a form of apprenticeship and self-directed study more than reading a book or working with a set of recipes and instructions someone else has put down. Remember, you are building and working with relationships between you and other living consciousnesses, and that process is always organic and unique to the parties involved. Further, you're building partnerships and alliances which by their nature honor and benefit all the participants.

From the information I've given in these Field Notes plus material in the Field Notes yet to come, you could certainly design your own self-study program in engaging with subtle worlds. If you do, I highly recommend you not go it alone but have a buddy, an empathetic and sympathetic friend, to whom you can turn for reflection and perspective. This person need not be engaging subtle worlds himself or herself, and need not be particularly sensitive to such worlds and beings. But he or she does need to know you well enough to spot if you might be getting off the track and can give you honest, clear feedback that is also supportive. Don't pick someone who is fearful of what you're doing or who might try to argue you out of it. You want support, not opposition. But you also want peer review, so to speak, and honest observation of your process. In engaging with subtle worlds, two minds (at least) and two hearts are almost always better than one. I have my "buddies" who I turn to for reflection and review, and even after more than sixty years of experience, I still find them invaluable and necessary. No one is infallible. The need for supportive, honest feedback is always present.

Finally, if you wish to engage with instruction, Lorian—the spiritual educational foundation I helped start and through which I now teach along with others—offers self-study material and classes, all found on the Lorian website at www.lorian.org. The overall program of training lasts several months but is divided into classes which can be taken separately. All the information you need to participate, should you wish to do so, is on our website.

Field Notes Four:
Anatomy of a Contact

A friend and I meet nearly every week for coffee and a chat. Although we've known each other for years and the place where we meet is the same Starbucks coffee house near our homes, each time we get together is a unique experience. The circumstances are never exactly the same. In a similar manner, each contact with a non-physical being or subtle energy is unique in its details and its effects. John and I worked together for twenty-seven years. During the initial five years I was training with him, we met every day and sometimes more than once a day. Yet each time was different; each time had a flavor and energy all its own. To make generalizations about such contacts is to risk running afoul of their uniqueness.

On the other hand, after over sixty years of engaging with non-physical beings, there are a few things that I feel safe in saying that will hold true for the majority of these contacts, just as there are things that I can say about the times my friend and I get together that will be true for every time we meet. I think of these as an anatomy of a contact.

Any being—any sentient entity on any level of existence, including physical persons like you and me—is essentially an energy field. To be more precise, each being is a multi-layered, multi-leveled energy field, uniquely configured and possessing an internal integrity and coherency. From this perspective, an encounter between a physical person and a non-physical being is a matter of bringing their individual energy systems into resonance without compromising each other. If the non-physical being is from one of the higher-order worlds and carries a more powerful or intense energy field—or if its energy field is very differently configured from that of a human—care has to be taken not to overload or disrupt the energy field of the incarnate person by impacting it with too much or too different an energy. The whole issue of engaging subtle worlds can be seen as an exercise in energy mechanics—a kind of metaphysical electrical engineering.

This may seem a cold way to look at it, and it certainly leaves out the personal and loving elements, but I find it helps as a way of understanding some of what is involved in engaging with the subtle realms. Even more, I think it may help to demystify or deglamorize the process. From my point of view, all inner beings are simply other kinds of lifeforms living in their own environments and interacting with each other, just as organisms and lifeforms do here in the physical world.

Part of the challenge in contacting and working with the subtle realms lies in our attitudes, particularly in what might be called the "halo effect." This can occur when a subtle being is glamorized simply because it *is* a non-physical being or when the energy of that being affects us in a way that makes us feel very good (or conversely, very bad). This latter would be the equivalent of meeting a physical person who is either very beautiful or handsome or ugly. In either case, people tend to treat such a person differently than normal because of the effect of their appearance, overlooking the actual quality of their nature. Thus, a handsome con man may get away with his deception because of the effect of his physical beauty, whereas a loving, compassionate, spiritual person may be disregarded if he is ugly.

Religious beliefs or mythic archetypes can play a role here as well. If we think of an angel not as a species of life, just as we are a species of life as well, but as a heavenly messenger from God, this can influence our response to it. We forget that we can be messengers from God, too. We may project more onto the angel by way of expectation and reverence than is deserved or helpful. The physical equivalent of this is when we give undue credence or authority to a person because he's wearing a uniform or is decorated with medals. Not that the uniform or the medals are unimportant; they may mean something significant. But by themselves they don't change the nature of that person or make him an extraordinary or special human being. The uniform or medals, in other words, are not a substitute for the innate character or quality of the person wearing them. A scoundrel can wear a uniform or medals while a saint might not. We should always honor and respect that which is honorable and worthy, but it's not always easy to go beyond the surface, either of appearance or of our projections, to see where that worthiness lies.

Transdimensional communication is different and challenging enough without complicating it with glamour or projections based on thought forms, beliefs, and projections. Respecting and even revering subtle beings, particularly those from the higher-order realms whose presence is so profoundly spiritual, is appropriate. Worshiping them or giving over one's power or sovereignty to them because of who or what we may think them to be is not. It destroys the possibility of partnership and diminishes the identity of the human being, something the truly spiritual beings seek to prevent and avoid.

It was for this reason that John often went to some lengths to help me see that I was an energy manifestation dealing with other energy manifestations in the form of various kinds of beings and thought forms existing in the non-physical dimensions. He wanted me to see this contact and communication as something natural and to approach it in the same attitude of naturalness that I would bring to any human communication. "What is important," he would say, "is the nature of the energy field you are contacting and how it flows and interacts with your own. Whether the being you're in contact with is an angel, a nature spirit, or something else is not necessarily the most important thing. What is important is the nature of the energy and blessing that emerges from the meeting and possible joining of your energies."

None of this, of course, takes away from the love that all involved in transdimensional contact can give to each other or experience in each other's presence. We may all be energy systems, but we are much more besides.

In my experience, there are four distinct energy phenomena involved in any contact with subtle beings. One is the complexity and nature of the particular configuration of a being's energy system.

This configuration is what makes any being an individual; it's that being's unique energy signature or "note." It's who the being is.

Sometimes I think of this as the "flavor" or "texture" of a being. It's as if every being is like a wine with its own particular aroma, color, consistency, and flavor. This represents the particular way this being metabolizes and combines energies within its overall field, just as a wine reflects the way particular grapes metabolized the natural elements of sun, soil, and water.

The second form of energy manifestation in an encounter is a result of the quantity of energy involved. How intensely or powerfully is a being radiating? The "flavor" of a being and its effect is not necessarily comparable to its radiance. There are nature spirits that I've encountered, for instance, that do not put forth a great deal of energy but in their non-humanness their "flavor" is very different. In contact with them, their radiant energy is easy to handle but the difference of their nature can be challenging.

On the other hand, John radiated a powerful energy that could be felt by others even when they couldn't see him, but the quality of his energy was very loving and compatible. It felt human and familiar. The real challenge comes when you engage with a being who is both very powerful and very different. Some nature devas are an example of this.

The transitional realms exist to mediate some of these differences and provide intermediary forms that some of the very powerful higher-order beings may use to step down their energy. It's also why such beings may create temporary shapes in the imaginal realm in order to mitigate some of the energy differences.

The third energy phenomenon is that of the contact itself. The very act of crossing dimensions and bringing and blending different energy systems together generates energy, sometimes quite a bit of it. This in itself can give rise to glamour or a halo effect. The actual act of contact can create a heightening of energy that can be pleasurable or exciting. It can surround the event with an energetic "glow" that can make the subtle being or what it has to say seem more powerful, charismatic, or meaningful than it really is.

This is not an unusual phenomenon. We experience it with

each other on the physical plane. Meeting someone in the excitement and ambience of a fancy restaurant or nightclub or in the midst of a celebration can create a very different impression of that person than we might have meeting them in ordinary circumstances on the street or in the workplace. The glamour of the setting or circumstance can rub off on a person. It's why shipboard romances can feel so powerful yet prove deceptive when the lovers are back on land and in ordinary circumstances.

In my experience, these three energy phenomena are present in every engagement with the subtle worlds in one degree or another. They can be very mild and have little impact upon your own energy field, or they can be very powerful and awe inspiring, or anything in between. Being aware of them and learning to integrate their effects, though, is part of the skill of engaging with the subtle worlds.

There is a fourth energy that's involved as well. That's the energy that comes from us. What we bring to the encounter makes a difference and helps to shape the engagement.

My energy state at the time a contact with a non-physical being takes place can affect the tenor and quality of that communication. This is not an unfamiliar principle. It happens all the time in everyday conversation. We can have the same conversation, but if I'm in a happy mood and feeling upbeat, I may hear you and take in the information differently than if I'm depressed or angry or distracted. This effect, though, can be magnified when working with inner beings for whom the exchange of energy is often more important and significant than the exchange of words.

This situation can be mediated by the subtle being. Often if I was worried or feeling agitated, John would approach me with an energy that was calming and loving, helping my own energy to become more serene. But he couldn't do it all. I had to take responsibility for and manage my own mental and emotional states as well.

The point is that if we see engagement and communication with subtle beings as an exchange between dynamic energy systems, then the state of our energy is vitally important as part of this process. This is one reason that attunement to self is one of the four basic practices that John recommended. I want to be able to understand myself well enough and have enough skill and control over my moods that I can enter and maintain a spirit of calmness and peace of mind when I need to, not just when engaging with subtle beings but at any time in my life.

This is also why John recommended that one's life be broad and rich with different types of experiences, rather than narrow and constrained by familiarity and habit, for the encounter with difference and variety trains one's energy field in being supple and adaptable.

It isn't just inner beings that carry different energies. Nature does as well in the form of different landscapes and environments. You could take advantage of this by visiting different parts of the country or even just different places around where you live. Likewise, if there's an opportunity to travel and visit different cultures and encounter different ideas and philosophies, do so as well. If you live near a large city, you can find ethnic neighborhoods to visit without having to go to other countries. Learning to engage and communicate with people who are different from you and not part of your familiar culture or way of thinking can not only enrich your life but teach you how to adapt to and handle different qualities of energy. It's not a matter of deciding which culture or way of thinking is right or wrong; you're not comparing them with your own in that sense. Rather you're learning to handle the energy of difference and to appreciate that which is different from yourself.

When I come into contact with a subtle being, then, the three types of energy that the being brings interact with the quality of energy I'm bringing to the encounter. The resulting mix may be gentle and mild; it could be volatile and difficult, or it could be anything in-between. Whatever it is, it will be unique to that encounter. Likewise, whatever that mix may be, the skill of transdimensional contact lies in being able to hold and to integrate this combination of energies in a balanced manner.

There are two other aspects to every contact. Each time we engage with a non-physical being there is a short-term and a long-term effect. Of course, this is true for nearly every experience we have, whether with subtle beings or physical ones. There's the effect of the experience in the moment, but then there are consequences and effects that may be more long lasting.

Again, as with energy phenomena, these effects may be mild and essentially negligible or they may be powerful and life-changing, and everything in-between.

The context for this is that nothing occurs in a vacuum. We are all, whether on this world or another dimension of consciousness, part of larger wholes. The events and experiences of my life are part of the overall pattern and unfoldment of my incarnation, which itself emerges from the larger context of my soul and its purposes and evolution; but my soul itself is part of larger patterns, such as the evolution of humanity and the unfoldment of the life of the World Soul, Gaia.

Many contacts with the higher-order worlds in particular have behind them the *holopoietic* impulse I wrote about earlier and may be part of a larger movement or campaign to help the physical world and humanity and to bring greater wholeness to the planetary system itself. This was certainly true for John and his colleagues. Even though much of our contact together was focused at first on my training and then on the specific work we did together, such as helping the development of the Findhorn Foundation community in northern Scotland, always in the background was the larger purpose of serving the intent of the World Soul to achieve greater wholeness.

A contact with a non-physical being can be an exciting, glamorous, high-energy event in a person's life, but it is only one event in the much larger context of his or her incarnation. One difference I've found between a being who is truly spiritual in nature and expression and one that is simply non-physical (though still benign, friendly and wishing to be helpful) is that the former takes into account the larger context and wholeness of one's life—that is to say, the long-term consequences of the contact—whereas the latter may not and may be more focused on the effects in the moment.

For example, I am married and have four children. I am embedded in a web of family responsibilities. I am also responsible to those with whom I work, to the work itself, and to a wide circle of friends and allies. I have on occasion run into subtle beings who carry an intense energy of momentum and urgency, following a particular task or quest. Such beings may desire me to help them and drop everything I'm doing and focus on their project, no matter what effect this might have on my human relationships, my family, my work, or my life as a whole. The contact is focused on the effects in the moment but disregards the larger, long-term context and consequences.

There are situations where this might be appropriate. If a neighbor runs into my house and yells "Drop whatever you're doing and get out! There's a gas leak and your house may explode!" (an event that really did happen some years ago), then it behooves me to listen and take action. But if a person shows up at my door and says, "I have this great opportunity for you and me to make a lot of money, but it means you'll have to move to another city and take up a different job," I'm more than happy to send that person on his way. The potential (and quite likely imaginary) benefits this person offers are not worth the disruption and chaos following him would bring to my family, my work, and my friends. And though this example sounds far-fetched, I've had similar things happen over the years with individuals who are convinced their projects are so important and world-altering that I should drop whatever else I'm doing and help them, thereby displaying both ignorance and unconcern about the larger patterns of my life and the responsibilities I hold.

Situations such as this are usually easily spotted when they happen on the physical level between incarnate persons, but they can be more, well, subtle and less obvious when they are part of a contact with a non-physical being, in part because of the glamour such contacts can engender in the moment. The larger picture and the long-term consequences can be lost in the excitement and energy of the moment.

This was an important issue for John. It was one reason he said at the very beginning of our time together, "You must always feel free to say no to me, whatever I may ask or suggest. If you cannot say no, you are not free in our relationship, and no partnership can develop between us. This holds true for any being from the inner, no matter how exalted or revered it may seem to you. You can always say no."

It was also why he stressed the importance of an individual's personality and incarnation. "Your task in this life," he said, "is to honor and develop your personality as a tool of love and wholeness, not to dismiss or dispose of it. It is an integral part of your incarnation and has a function and role to perform. A truly spiritual contact may ask you to put your personality into the perspective of a larger wholeness but it will not ask you to damage or ignore it."

Similarly, he said, "an incarnation is the extension of a soul and emerges from love. Honor it as something holy, for it is. It is your soul's gift to the struggles of this world."

The longer term context, then, of any contact with the subtle worlds is the integrity, wholeness, and coherent unfoldment of our incarnation, our personality, and our individuality and of their capacity to be a blessing within the world. All contacts take place within that context. They also take place within the larger context of the World Soul, the love that it bears for all life, and the needs it has to be whole in its own being and expression. These larger contexts need to be remembered and honored, even in the excitement of the moment as we deal with the energies and ideas a contact brings.

Field Notes Five:
Mapping the Subtle Realms

When John first came to me, he said that he wished to help me become more familiar with the subtle worlds and to learn to navigate them. This was exciting news. However, having just left college, I was still thinking in academic terms. I imagined John was going to give me geography lessons outlining the territory of the subtle worlds. I confess that in those days, I thought of these realms as discrete places the same way I thought of Ohio, San Francisco or Australia. I expected John to provide me with something like an atlas or a Michelin guide. The reality was very different.

I came to realize very quickly that the subtle worlds were not so much places in the physical sense but conditions and states of consciousness. While many of them could *look* like ordinary places complete with landscapes and buildings, they were in fact manifestations of thought and life. Perhaps a more accurate way of putting it is that they are locations within the vast, universal spectrum of life and sentiency. Or to use an earlier analogy, they are like notes on a guitar string. The plucking of the string creates and sustains the note.

As far as I can tell, in most instances the activity that brings a subtle realm into being, gives it form, structure and organization, and maintains it arises from the World Soul or from collectives of beings gathered together to manifest and experience a particular environment and condition of consciousness. It is their energy and intentionality that does the "plucking," though it is the Sacred—the Generative Mystery—that provides (indeed, in some ways *is*) the "guitar string," the primal substance from which all things emerge or are created. Environments are in a magical way exuded or secreted by the life process of the beings that live in them, a process that creates an overwhelming variety of "places."

In some specific instances, certain places within the non-physical realms are created and held in existence by a particular Being for a specific purpose or as an act of service.

Because of this, John didn't travel to locations as much as he traveled to specific Beings. The "roads" we traveled were pathways of life and consciousness, as well as of energy. For example, many people who journey into the subtle worlds report the existence of something like a "Hall of Records" or a vast Library where information may be found. When John wished to go to such a place, he didn't go to the Library, however, he went to the Librarian, the Being whose consciousness was creating or ensouling this place and who had a unique energy signature. It was that energy signature, like the beacon from a lighthouse or the broadcast from a radio station, that John taught me to home in on as a way of drawing my consciousness into the presence and vicinity or environment of that particular being.

Travel itself was more a phenomenon of relationship and resonance than it was one of movement across space over some distance. In fact, distances as such didn't seem to exist in the same way in the subtle worlds as they do here on earth. How near or far something or someone might be was a function of resonance and affinity, of how well you knew them and felt connected to them. The deeper and more loving the relationship between you, the closer you are.

Other factors were involved as well. One of these was the amount of energy it took to bridge the difference between one state of consciousness and another. Every condition of being or state of consciousness exists as a particular energy state, as I have said. If you and I are similar in our state of being, the energy difference—the energetic differential—between us is very small. It would be as if we were standing on the same level of ground. But if we are very different—if you, say, were an archangel existing in a very high energy state—then the energy differential would be much greater. It would be as if you were standing on a high hill and I was at its base.

There might not be much actual physical *distance* between us "as the crow flies" but I have to perform much more work and expend more energy to climb the hill to be next to you, or you would have to do that to descend the hill to meet me. There is an energy distance between us. If I don't have the strength to climb the hill and you can't descend it easily to reach me, then we are separated as much as if we were in different cities.

Many subtle beings, particularly in the higher-order worlds, live "up the hill" from us. In the last set of Field Notes, I spoke of the energies involved in contact with non-physical entities. One of these, the energy of the contact itself, is the result of the energy differentials. Imagine if you are at the top of a hill and I'm at the bottom, and you come running down to meet me. You build up kinetic energy in doing so as you diminish the height between us, and if I have to catch you, I have to handle not only your mass but also all the energy you've built up running down the hill. If I'm not braced properly (I call this "standing in sovereignty"), you can knock me over. In contact terms, I'm overwhelmed by the energy that accompanies your engagement with me. In this sense, you as the inner being may appear to me to have much more energy than you really do in your natural state, just as you, the physical person running down the hill, bring much more energy with you due to the momentum you build up than if we met at an equal level standing next to each other.

In the beginning of this training with John, the subtle worlds seemed to me not at all like the orderly, hierarchically-layered diagrams I had seen in esoteric texts. If anything, they reminded me of the Amazonian rainforest, a blooming, confusing mass of life. At first it seemed hopeless that I could find my way around them, just as I would feel lost if I were dropped into the jungle. I let John know several times that what I really wanted was a map.

John's response to this desire was, "When it comes to the subtle worlds, you need to create your own map."

When I think of the town in which I live, my mental map of it is very different from the generic street map handed out by the Chamber of Commerce. My internal town map is organized around my favorite places, the bookstores, theaters, and restaurants I favor, and where my friends' homes are located. After some years living here, I know shortcuts and backstreet ways to get from one place to another, avoiding the main roads. It is indeed less a map of locations and more a map of my relationships with people and places in the town where I live.

In my experience, the nature of the subtle realms is so relational that no one else's map, however well drawn and detailed, will be the same as your own, any more than your neighbor has the same experiences and relationships as you do with the town in which you live. Your map is a description of your relationships. Someone else's description, while potentially helpful in some regards, may lead you astray if you try to apply it literally to your own experiences.

But it's not all purely subjective. If I superimpose my map on the one the Chamber of Commerce offers, which is basically a street map such as one might get at a neighborhood service station, I would find many points in common. The main streets of my town divide the town into major areas, and that's a useful orientation for me, too. Those divisions are part of my internal mental map as well. I think, "Oh, that store's north of Gilmore Street" or "my friends live west of Front Street." These main streets would have a place on my map also.

These main streets also help define functions in my town. There's the downtown where theaters and the public buildings like city hall, the police station and the library are located; there's the shopping district where most of the stores and restaurants are, and there are the residential areas where people live. My personal mental map of my town makes note of these functional districts as well.

My map of my town is a blend of my personal, subjective experiences and relationships with people and places in the town and the geographical street map provided by the Chamber of Commerce. This is true for the ways I map the subtle worlds as well. I find my way around by the relationships I've formed, which are personal to me. But there are also "streets" and regions, energy pathways and boundaries, that over the millennia have been experienced and recognized by most men and women who have "walked between the worlds," irrespective of their culture or background. My division of the subtle worlds into the incarnate realms, the transitional realms, and the higher-order realms is a simple expression of the existence of these boundaries and regions. Much more complex divisions and maps are possible.

In my classes, I often discuss and use these more complex maps. Certain kinds of work with the subtle realms benefit from greater precision in one's mapping. I will mention some of these as we go along in these Field Notes, but on the whole, the three-fold map I've already offered you is perfectly adequate for purposes of introduction and basic orientation.

The point I wish to make in this set of Field Notes, though, is that there are many possible ways of mapping the subtle worlds, just as there are different ways of mapping my town. I can map my town by its geography and the layout of its streets. I can map it by the services it provides. I can map it by its schools or by its stores, by its restaurants or by the geographical features such as a stream, a lake, foothills, and so forth that all exist within its city limits. Each map will highlight a particular feature or set of relationships, and each map will leave something out. Each type of map will be good for some purposes and lacking for others. This is true for the subtle worlds as well.

For instance, think of a theater company. There are the actors who go on stage and present the plays to the public. There are the behind-the-scenes crew who make the sets, keep the theater in good order, prepare costumes, and so on. Then there are those who serve the wellbeing and development of the company, who see that there are salaries and health insurance, who make sure meals are provided when needed, and who decide what plays will be performed, commission new plays to be written, advertise, and basically attend to the integration, coherency and well-being of the company as a whole.

A similar kind of division of labor can be found within Gaia's planetary system. There are those who are incarnated, who are living out the plays and are the equivalent of the actors and actresses of the theater. They are part of what I think of as the Incarnate Sphere, those who live out and express the ideas and intentionalities of the soul, whether this is an individual soul or the world soul. David Spangler, for instance, began as an idea in the consciousness of my soul, and my incarnation is the living out (the acting out in my metaphor) of that idea.

Then there are those who take care of the theater, so to speak, who build and maintain the props, the scenery, the costumes — that is to say, the forms, patterns, and structures that make the planet what it is and help it exist and function. These beings, who include nature spirits and devas but also certain kinds of angelic beings, are part of what I think of as the Planetary or Formative Sphere of activity.

Finally, those who take care of the well-being, development, and spirit of the theater company of earth are those beings, generally in the higher-order worlds, who embody, mediate and see to the circulation of spiritual energies. I see them as making up the Spiritual Sphere of activity.

So I could draw a map of the subtle worlds and the beings within them based on which sphere I felt they represented. Such a map would be based more on function than locality. For instance, actors might usually be found on stage, but they could also be in their dressing rooms or back stage waiting to go on; they might be helping out with props and costuming, and they might be involved with advertising and overall planning for the theater's future seasons. Yet wherever they were, they would still be bringing to bear the consciousness and perspective of being an actor.

Similarly, those beings who have taken on the task of incarnating or manifesting and expressing the ideas in the mind of Gaia or Humanity may be found in physical bodies, in the post-mortem realms, in higher-order worlds, or in the transitional realms helping currently embodied individuals, depending on where they were in the cycle of their incarnations and how they were helping out.

These three spheres of activity — Incarnation, Formative, and Spiritual — provide one possible way of mapping; they also overlap with each other, for whatever the map may be, the actual territory is an undivided wholeness. In the subtle realms as on the earth, we need to remember, the map is *not* the territory.

There is another way of mapping that I'm going to use for the remainder of these Field Notes. This might be called "mapping by energy." Or using the metaphor of the hill I described earlier, I might call it "mapping by height." In effect, we're going to start with the part of the subtle worlds that is closest to us in energy—nearest to us on the hill—and work our way upslope.

This way mimics how we might learn to engage with the subtle worlds, as well as how we do so on a regular basis in our everyday lives. We start with what is closest to us and easiest to contact and work with and work our way towards that which is further away (in terms of energy differential) and potentially harder to work with.

In so doing, the place we begin is with life.

Field Notes Six:
Life

When I was five or six years old, my parents and I went to see a movie that included a Walt Disney cartoon. In this animated short feature, the furniture and other objects were all alive and talked to the characters. I remember sitting in the dark watching this, thinking, "Someone's made a movie about *my* world." Not that sofas and chairs got up and sang and danced in my world as they did in the Disney cartoon (although, I must admit, that would have been pretty cool). They didn't carry on extended conversations with me. But they definitely had a presence, a sentient energy of which I was aware. And interaction between me and that sentiency was possible.

The idea that everything is alive has been part of the shamanic world view for millennia, and in more recent history can be found in some religious mystical traditions as well. The pervasiveness of life is something individuals in all cultures and times have experienced. Even in popular language and culture, we invest our things with personalities and talk about them as if they were alive. Modern science and psychology would say this is merely anthropomorphic projection on our part, but older wisdoms would see this differently. And now there are branches of complexity theory and the science of nonequilibrium thermodynamics that are broadening our definition of what is life beyond the boundaries of biology and organic chemistry.

As shamanic ideas have become more present in our culture, particularly among those who explore and practice alternative and nature-oriented spiritualities, and we have become more holistically and ecologically minded, the phrase "Everything is alive" has become more common. But what exactly does it mean? What is this life that everything shares? A mystic might say that it's God's Life or "Universal Life," but just what does that mean when applied to metal and plastic or to the upholstery of my favorite sofa? No one, I think, would claim it's the same as the life that animates you and me, the birds outside my window, or the trees in which they are nesting.

Yet all my life I have experienced everything around me as alive. Or put another way, life to me is not just a biological or organic phenomenon. It is an energy manifestation that is organized and self-sustaining, an eddy or vortex within a larger flow of universal energy. What does this mean?

To explore this question, I'd like to share with you how I experience the presence of life within an inanimate object, something normally considered nonliving. For this purpose I choose a sofa in my living room as my example. As much as I am able to translate a subtle experience into words, I shall describe this process phenomenologically, much as a naturalist might describe his experience of a new species of animal or plant.

The first thing I see when I look at my sofa is what anyone would see: its surface appearance. It's a tad over seven feet in length, just perfect for lying down on to watch television (assuming I get to it before one of my kids does). It's made of wood and cloth and a thick upholstered padding, with equally thick, soft cushions. It's red in color with alternating stripes of gold and green against a background pattern of leaves and vines. It's lovely to look at and very comfortable. And at this level of perception, it's very ordinary and not at all "living" in any normal sense of that word.

If I shift my awareness to a deeper level, the sofa becomes something more. At the simplest level "inward," I am aware of an energy field surrounding it. All things are surrounded by this aura of energy. It's part of the subtle field of the incarnational realms. This field is "sticky" and can accumulate other forms of energy, such as those generated by our thoughts and emotions but also by our spiritual attunements. For example, if I'm content and peaceful when I sit or lie upon the sofa, the vibration of that peace can enter its energy field and stick there, particularly if it's a consistent experience over time; likewise, if I'm agitated and upset, those emotional energies can be caught. It's as if there's a layer of psychic Velcro around the sofa that catches and holds energetic "lint" from the mental, emotional, and spiritual activity in the environment.

If certain of these psychic energies are repeated over and over, they can become deeply impressed upon the energy field of the sofa, going more deeply into its energetic substance than just this surface "Velcro" layer I'm describing. But otherwise, this energy "lint" is lightly held and can easily be removed through some practice of energy hygiene or cleansing. Just doing one's housework with love and in a cheerful manner—especially with the vibration of music—while visualizing clean, clear, vital energy sweeping through the room and the furniture can usually wipe such stuff away.

Sensing this level of subtle energy can give a psychic or energetic impression of life, but it's really the life energy of others "recorded" on the subtle substance of the sofa. At this simple level, the sofa is energetically active and responsive, as most things are, but this is not the same as being alive. To discover how the sofa itself is alive, I must go deeper.

As I shift my awareness to do this, it's possible I may "overshoot" the mark and find myself slipping into a mystical state in which I become aware of a Presence and Life that is not just within the sofa but within all things. This is the primal Life from which all creation is emerging, and I think of it as the level of the Sacred. This Life is a universal condition. It's the Life we all share, the Life of the Cosmos, the Life of the One, however we may understand that.

At this level, the sofa is most definitely alive, but it's no longer a sofa. It's part of a universal oneness flowing through all things, underlying the manifestation of all things. I might as well say the Cosmos is alive and leave it at that.

In astronomy, there's a concept called *the habitable zone* which is the distance from a star at which a planet could have conditions favorable to the existence and evolution of life such as we know it. How large this zone is and where it is found in a solar system depends on the nature and characteristics of that system's star. Astronomers sometimes call this the "Goldilocks Zone" because it's neither too hot nor too cold but "just right."

In a similar way, when I look for the life within the sofa, if I don't look far enough, I remain at the level of surface appearance or at the level of its aura with its accumulation of energy. In a sense, this is "too cold." If I look too far or go too deep, I enter a realm of Life that is vast, cosmic, and all-pervading, the Life of the One. This, by contrast, is "too hot."

So what I seek is the "Goldilocks Zone of Life," and I find it in the way in which the universal flow of life becomes organized around specific "attractors" to form patterns, systems, and vortices of energy that are persistent and self-sustaining to some degree. To me, these are all *incarnational* systems. They don't just accumulate energy or substance; they organize it in some persistent manner; they are *autopoietic* or self-creating. They possess some level of coherency and integration. In my terminology, they possess *identity* and they also have a boundary of some nature that separates them from the rest of the energy flowing around them.

Imagine a river. As it flows, a branch lies across the river bank and into the water, and where it dips into the river, it impedes or restrains that flow to some degree. The water becomes turbulent in the area around the branch; an eddy may form. This eddy is a shape, a presence that persists even though water flows through it as long as the branch is there forming a boundary to catch that flow.

In a way, life is like that eddy, a complex organization of flowing energy in and around a boundary condition analogous to the tree branch that defines its particularity and enables a system of organization to develop and persist.

So as I examine my sofa with a deeper perception, I come to an energy phenomenon that is not a universal presence or force and not just an accumulation of characteristics and energies from outside itself but one that has its own particular unique, internally coherent and integrated organization. This is where I experience the sofa as something living, not in a biological way but in an energetic way.

What is this life like as I perceive it?

To use the metaphor of the river again, the branch that created the eddy of energetic organization and life in this instance is the human intent and imagination that created the sofa. In the first instance, it's the idea of "sofa" itself which has a long lineage back to the original idea of a couch or bed; that's at the stem of this branch. But the specific twigs and leaves of the branch that are hanging into the flow of universal substance and creating the boundary that forms the eddy are the specific idea and design for this particular kind of sofa.

This creative intent forms the "attractor" around which energy begins to organize and pattern itself. It is the initial identity that combines with a boundary to form the incarnation of this sofa. This incarnation is not entirely the work of the designer who initially fashioned the sofa. He or she created the physical pattern—what the sofa looks like and what it's designed to do—but this is the branch dangling into the flow of the river which creates the boundaries around which the energy organization forms. The "eddy" or energy pattern itself that forms from this "branch" is different. The two are related but they are not identical.

The energy pattern of the sofa at this "Goldilocks" level doesn't look to me like a sofa at all. In fact it doesn't "look" like anything in particular; rather it is a "consciousness shape" that reflects the complexity and patterning of the energy organization itself. Its shape reflects its capacities and potentials of consciousness. I don't know how to describe this in a physical way; what, after all, is the "shape" of a mathematical equation or of a musical melody?

When I experience this "shape" of organized energy that is my sofa, it is not terribly complex or flexible; it cannot take much initiative, for instance (and none at all on a physical level). A human being, by comparison, is immensely more complex, organized, and capable as an energy form.

To use a different metaphor entirely, toy action figures are classified by "points of articulation," that is, by the joints that they possess, which determines where they can bend and how flexible they are. As a kid I had a set of rubber toy soldiers that were each molded as a single piece. They had no points of articulation and could not bend at all. Then toy makers developed toy soldiers that had one point of articulation; they could bend at the waist. Later they made figures that could turn their heads or move their hands or feet, their elbows or knees. They had more points of articulation, more joints, and the more they had, the more they could be posed in the various positions that a real person could take. You didn't have to imagine that your toy soldier was kneeling or bending or sitting; he really could kneel, bend, or sit.

Human beings energetically have an immense number of "points of articulation" or "joints of sentiency;" these are the many ways our consciousnesses can "bend" and configure to the environment, take initiative, create, and so on. My sofa has only a few joints of sentiency, and thus it is much more limited as an energy being than I am in what it can perceive and do. Yet it is not totally unaware or inanimate at this energetic level.

I perceive that at this "Goldilocks" level an organization of sentient energy exists in my sofa. It is aware and alive, though not in the way that I am or that any organic, biological being is. It is this organization and presence of sentiency that I experienced as a child and felt as the life within the furniture and other objects that made up my world, so charmingly and whimsically portrayed in the Disney cartoon.

I think of this organization of sentient energy as an "incarnation." It embodies an identity, however simple it might be; it possesses boundaries that define it and distinguish it from its environment; it connects and engages with its environment in interactive ways. I experience this organization of energy as living. It exists in the subtle field of the incarnate realms with a capacity for some degree of awareness, response, and evolution.

It may be very simple life, and the life around my sofa certainly is, but it is still life. It is a presence of sentiency.

So what does this mean?

Well, what it doesn't mean is that my sofa is suddenly going to get up and cavort around the room. I'm not going to come out one morning and discover that the sofa and my easy chair have been having a relationship and are now the proud parents of twin footrests. We're not talking biology here.

To clarify what we are talking about, let me define life a little further. I think of life as a dynamic organization of energy of sufficient complexity, coherency, integrity, flow, and interaction with its environment that sentiency can manifest and through it consciousness can evolve.

When I look around me at the things in my world and say, "Everything is alive," what I'm really saying is that everything is consciousness in a process of evolution. Just as evolutionary biologists look at a human being and say, "Millions of years ago, you were just a single cell swimming in a primeval sea," so I might look at myself and think, "Millions of years ago, my consciousness was a sofa in an alien's living room circling Epsilon Beta IV in the Gamma Quadrant!" And who knows what far future David Spangler may be starting his evolution of consciousness as my easy chair right now?

This is fanciful, of course, but my main point is not. We all participate in a universe of consciousness that is evolving all the time, from the dimmest flickering of sentiency existing in a dream state that is not even self-aware to the fabulously and unimaginably complex and radiant cosmic Beings whose lives embrace entire galaxies. And what we do affects that evolution, at least in the environment around us.

I have encountered subtle beings in the higher-order realms in comparison to whom my consciousness is not much more evolved than the sentiency I find in my sofa. Their response to me is always loving, caring, considerate, and appropriate. They are like shepherds of consciousness, tending its evolution across vast expanses of life and energy. The light of my sentiency is like a shadow compared to theirs, yet they tend to it—as they do to millions and billions of other lives and consciousnesses within the field of their awareness—as if it were the brightest, most valuable flame in creation.

This is the true implication of saying that everything is alive. We are each caretakers for the consciousnesses evolving around us, particularly those of lesser complexity and capacity than our own. When it gets down to it, I really am my sofa's keeper!

When I tune in to that level of energetic organization in and around my sofa capable of holding a flame of sentiency—the level of organization that I perceive as the life within the sofa—I'm aware of a presence. It's not very complex or aware. A single cell has more awareness than this presence. But when I direct my attention to it and send love to it, I'm aware that it responds. It's like blowing upon a coal which then brightens and flares up with heat and light. It soaks the love up and the energy shifts within its organization. It becomes a little more active, a little more complex. In a sense it "speeds up." If I do this overtime as a regular practice, the energy life within the sofa becomes more aware, more active in its own sphere of being. It is able to participate more in the energy life around it. This simple sentiency evolves and becomes more responsive.

In effect, my energy, my consciousness, my attention shapes the energy environment and organization of this simple level of life. I can through my love and awareness heighten its evolution or I can through more negative emotions dampen it. And when I heighten and foster it through my love, I discover that this life becomes more aware and can send love and energy back. This can be very practical. By loving the things in my environment, I awaken the life within them to love me in return. In a real way, I am teaching them about love and how to love, not in any philosophical way but through a form of stimulus and response. This is one of the powerful things we can do when we expand our attention and awareness to embrace the field of subtle energies immediately around us.

As the life in my things is exposed to the complex vibrations of the love a human being can offer, it grows in its capacity to respond. To the extent it is able, given its energetic organization and awareness, this life and consciousness can send energy and love back to me. I'm not talking about the depth or complexity of energy and love that a plant, an animal, or a human could offer me, but it's still love, however simple it may be, and that counts for something. It can become a meaningful part of my everyday life, a nourishing part of my energy environment.

Even though the level of consciousness in most of our things is very basic and its light only a small spark, if human creativity, will, effort, and love have gone into its creation, then the item may have a more evolved energy organization and thus more life and consciousness than normal. It's one of the energetic qualities that distinguishes hand-made items and fine art from machine-made copies or items that are mass-produced. We can feel this, even if we're not sure what we're sensing.

If the organization of energy and life becomes complex enough, another phenomenon may occur. The object may become a point of contact—a kind of partial incarnation—for a non-physical entity which itself may be significantly more advanced and aware. If this were to happen to my sofa, then when I tuned into it, I might find myself in contact with a subtle being, most likely from the transitional realms, that would be quite capable of engaging and communicating with me.

When my first child was about five or so, we took a trip to Disneyland where I bought him a stuffed animal. It was *Bumblelion*, a creature that was part bumblebee and part lion, the star of a popular Disney cartoon series on television at the time. It was so whimsical and cute, I couldn't resist it, and John-Michael fell in love with it. It went everywhere with him; he slept with it, he ate with it, he played with it.

One day I was holding Bumblelion and became aware of a presence around it. As it turned out, it was a kind of playful spirit that was also partly a protector. It was one of a class of beings—I suppose one could think of them as guardian spirits—that regularly associate with children. This one had attached itself to the energy of Bumblelion. Johnny had poured so much love into this stuffed animal that its own energy organization had become complex enough and energetic enough, that this inner being could see it and connect to it. It was using this stuffed toy as a point of physical connection to our world through which its own loving and protective energies could flow to my son.

After that, when I would buy a stuffed animal for one of my children or for the children of friends, I would make a point of energizing the toy with love and then reaching out to one of these beings to invite it to connect with that energy and make that toy a point of contact to better bless the child who would be using it. They became stuffed talismans!

Beings of this nature form associations with our things in order to have closer contact with human energies. They are evolving, too, and are also benefitted by our loving awareness. And their response can definitely help us in the evolution of our consciousnesses as well.

Being aware of the secret life of things—that, as a friend of mine says, every some*thing* is really a some*one*—makes me aware of how very much we are all part of a community. But I don't have to have that awareness in order to bless my environment with my love. I can be totally unaware of any level of life and consciousness within my sofa or any other piece of furniture and still give it love. That love will be felt and have an effect. I can also be a shepherd of consciousness even if I can't see the sheep.

Field Notes Seven:
Self

The place to start in developing an attunement to the subtle worlds is with life. As I suggested in the last set of Field Notes, from the perspective of the beings of the non-physical dimensions, everything is alive. Life is all-pervading, transcending our biological definitions of it. Subtle beings are themselves simply another form of life. If I learn to attune to life, then I'm laying the foundation for attuning to specific forms that life can take, even if those forms manifest on other dimensions than the physical world.

This is a point worth emphasizing. Sometimes too much attention is placed on the mechanics or the techniques of developing subtle perception, as if the organs of perception were more important than the act of perceiving. A good friend of mine who is deaf "hears" more in her silence about what's going on and what's important than many people who have perfectly good ears. She is a very spiritually attuned and loving person. Likewise, I have known blind people who see their world more deeply and profoundly than many sighted individuals because they are lovingly attuned to the world around them. Opening the fabled "third eye" sounds dramatic and exciting, but the object is really subtle awareness more than subtle perception. It is the ability to form relationships and partnering alliances with subtle beings, not simply seeing their forms, which may not be their real forms anyway.

In short, subtle awareness and perception is a way of honoring and participating in life and as such draws more on the power of an open and loving heart than it does on any particular psychic capacity.

With this in mind, I recommend beginning training in

subtle awareness and perception by expanding one's awareness and appreciation of life itself, beginning with the forms that are immediately apparent to us. We are each surrounded by living beings that are perfectly apparent to our physical senses. How do we honor them? How do we appreciate them? How do we respond to them? At times I have found individuals pursuing psychic phenomena and the development of subtle perception because they either can't or don't wish to make the effort to connect with the incarnated people in their lives. They're seeking out friendships beyond this world. There's nothing wrong with being friends with non-physical beings, but not, I feel, at the expense of or substitution for friendship and connection with physical people.

In my own life, I make it a practice to be as aware and acknowledging of the physical life around me as I can be. If I find an insect in my house that I don't feel should belong there, I take it outside, but in the process, I send it love and blessing for its life path. Like me, it's trying to fulfill its nature in the best way it can.

This acknowledgement goes beyond organic life. I say hello mentally to everything, whether it's animate or inanimate. This may sound silly, but it reminds me daily that life is everywhere and in everything and that contact with the unseen worlds is really an exercise in life awareness, not psychic awareness.

Taking this idea further, forming partnerships with the subtle worlds is also an exercise in love and respect. So I practice loving. Love doesn't have to take the form of emotional affection or passionate attraction. The simplest form of love is respect and honoring, so I honor everything around me to the best of my ability. I open my heart to my immediate world in appreciation and respect, and I find more times than not that this becomes a seed for a much deeper, more profound love to emerge—a love that responds in recognition within the other of a kindred spirit of sacredness, a love, in other words, born of the fellowship of life I share with all other beings. Whether it's my coffee cup, my computer desk, the pen on the desk, the spider crawling up the wall, the rose in a nearby vase, the ferrets sleeping downstairs in my daughter's bedroom, the trees outside my window, or anything or anyone else around me, all are manifestations, as am I, of a primal, living, sentient force. We are all expressions of the Sacred, and that is truly worthy of love.

I was trained from the perspective that development of subtle awareness begins with practicing an awareness of and a respect and love for life in its myriad manifestations. This is the essence of the second practice John recommended to me. I called it attunement to the Sacred, which for John was a presence innately in all things. It is the foundation on which to stand while reaching out to the infinite wonder and vastness of life within the unseen worlds.

Standing on that foundation, where do we go next? What do we reach out to?

The answer may surprise you. You reach out to yourself. You are your own subtle world. When we think of incarnation, we may think only of having bodies. But we have subtle aspects as well. We're not just physical bodies but minds, emotions, and vital energies. These capacities and qualities within us create energetic fields around us which in effect form a set of subtle bodies we can use for interaction with the subtle worlds.

This personal subtle world is important, for as I have said, the qualities of energy which it carries and holds directly affect and help to shape any contact we have with the inner worlds. A higher-order being can override these qualities if it needs to (if, for instance, we are depressed or angry and the subtle being is seeking to help us and communicate to us through the energy of that anger or depression), but this costs energy and is not always one hundred percent successful. Contact is much more successful if the energies within our personal subtle world—our "aura"—are harmonious and resonant with the energies of the being we seek to engage.

Obviously, the nature and focus of our thoughts and feelings, the things we habitually think about and the ways we habitually respond emotionally to events and people in our life, affect the quality of subtle energies we broadcast into our own subtle fields and from there into the world. This is why a practice of self-reflection can be important. We want to honestly know our habits of thought and feeling so that if necessary we can change and improve them. Negative and hurtful thinking and emotions, as a customary, *habitual* expression, will fill our personal subtle fields with equivalent negative energies which increase the possibility of attracting the wrong kind of subtle beings and attuning to the more dangerous places upon the inner. The occasional negative thought or emotion in the midst of a day where the bulk of our thinking and feeling is positive and loving will not have that effect.

The practice of acknowledging, appreciating, and loving life in all its forms is a practice that directly affects the quality of energies in our personal subtle world. All the four practices that John suggested do so in beneficial and positive ways.

We can begin our exploration into the subtle worlds by tuning into our own bodies. Each of our organs manifests its own subtle field of energy unique to its function and nature. There are many practices of spiritual development that make use of this fact by attuning to the heart which arguably might be seen as the center of life within our bodies.

But I have found it useful to go beyond that and attune to the cells that make up my body. There are more cells in each of our bodies than there are visible stars in the sky. Even more impressively, there are even more microbes and bacteria that live in and on our bodies than there are somatic or bodily cells themselves, and many of these microbes are absolutely essential to our health and wellbeing. In one sense, then, we are each "hive beings" or at least vast communities of life.

From my perspective, each of these cells or microbes is a living being in its own right, radiating its own subtle energy. It has sentiency and awareness. If I can appreciate and acknowledge the life in my sofa, as I described in the last set of Field Notes, I can certainly do so for one of the cells in my body (not to mention all of them together).

An interesting experiment in meditation and attunement, then, is to focus your respectful and loving attention onto a cell in your body that can represent all your cells and feel into its subtle energy and consciousness. Try to discern the felt sense of this cell. What is its energy like?

There exists in each of us a particular kind of subtle being that is associated with our bodies and their cells. I think of it as the collective consciousness or spirit of all the cells that make up our physical bodies. I call it the "body elemental." This being is formed out of the substance and energy field of the World Soul, Gaia, in response to the collective field created by the cells of the body and the associated microbes and bacteria. In a way, it inhabits and becomes part of and personifies that collective field. This body elemental, to the extent that it is able, works to keep our bodies whole and functioning well, though it has limits to what it can do and is not all-powerful. Certainly its work can be interfered with by the energies coming from our conscious thoughts and feelings, or conversely, it can be strengthened and empowered by our thoughts and feelings.

Attuning to and becoming acquainted with your body elemental is part of the practice of attuning to self and represents a way of engaging with a subtle being that is truly "up close and personal." It also provides a contact that we can work with to the benefit of our body and its health. I have found that asking my body elemental to protect and care for my cells and my health often boosts my immune system and keeps me healthy when others around me are coming down with colds or the flu, and if I do get sick, it can help with my healing and recovery. It's only one factor in the overall health of my body and there are limits on what it can do, but it's still an important subtle ally and one that's close at hand.

As a further step, you can also attune to your subtle energy field itself. You might think of this as the energetic atmosphere around your body, just as there's a gaseous atmosphere around the physical globe of the earth. And like the atmosphere of the earth, it has a complex structure with eddies, whirlpools of energy, currents, and the like.

The actual distance to which this field can extend around a body varies from person to person and from moment to moment. It can depend on circumstances, the environment you're in, whom you're with, and on just how much subtle energy you're pumping into it. If you're doing martial arts or an energy practice such as tai chi or qi gong and invoking subtle forces in the form of chi, your field may expand. If you're in a pleasant, relaxed setting, and you're having a good time, especially with someone you love and enjoy being with, your field can expand. If you're someplace you don't want to be where you feel pressure or unpleasant vibrations in the environment, or you're with someone you don't want to be with, your field can contract.

This personal subtle energy field is the closest subtle world to you and as such is a perfect place to practice developing your subtle awareness. Focus your relaxed and loving attention into this field just as earlier you focused it into a cell in your body. Imagine your consciousness extending from your physical body into this personal subtle field. What is the felt sense of this field or aura around you? What is the "atmosphere" of your personal "planet" like?

This subtle field can be an active and beautiful place. Many of the subtle energies that reach and impact us from various levels of the inner worlds can produce an effect here, much as a meteor entering the earth's atmosphere from space can produce a fiery show in the night sky. If I enter my aura with a still mind and heart and with a spirit of simply appreciating the energy that is around me and appreciating the beauty and function of this field, then I can sense a myriad of forces at work like musical tones or sparkling lights. Energies are arising from my cells, energies are bursting into my field from higher levels and from the physical environment around me. It is an interesting and active place.

One thing you can do when attuning to your personal subtle field is to deliberately attune to a source of Light and sacredness and draw its presence and energy into your field. You can fill this field with Light, with Love, and with other qualities that you draw from within yourself or from non-physical, transpersonal sources. In some ways, the energy that is within your personal subtle field is what nourishes and supports your body elemental, so filling your field with good vibrations is always a useful thing to do.

When I began working with John, one of the first things he did as part of my training was to introduce me to a new and deeper understanding of the self than I had had before. He wanted me to realize that Light and spiritual energy didn't just come from the higher-order worlds; it also came from each of us. From John's point of view, each person is a generating station of spiritual energy, and this generating station is located in the incarnate, personal self (including the personality), not just or exclusively on transpersonal or "spiritual" realms. Part of the training he gave me was to experience this for myself and learn to attune to it. I called this spiritual energy our *empersonal spirit*, meaning a spiritual force originating and emanating from the personal side of our nature and complementing what comes from the transpersonal parts of us such as our soul.

Back in the middle of the Sixties when John and I were first working together, John was satisfied simply for me to realize that this empersonal spirit existed as a spiritual "self-Light" that I could attune to that came from my personal self. Developing and nourishing this empersonal spirit and self-light was, as I have said earlier, part of what John meant by the first practice of attunement to self. Twenty-seven years later when John said goodbye and moved on to other realms and other kinds of work, though, he suggested I explore and research this self-light more fully.

In effect, this research has been the main focus of my explorations and communications with the subtle worlds over the past two decades, and I have formulated most of my observations and discoveries in a set of insights and practices I call *Incarnational Spirituality*. This is a much broader topic than I can cover in these Field Notes, but if you wish to investigate it more fully, I list ways to do so in the Resources section at the end of this book.

The main focus of this research, though, has been on the process of incarnation itself: the means by which the soul intentionally turns part of itself into a state of consciousness and a form that can manifest and function in a physical environment like the earth. In a way, this process has much in common with the phenomena involved in transdimensional contact and communication. After all, the soul, as I experience it, is a higher-order being, a hyperdimensional consciousness and energy structure existing in five or more dimensions. To incarnate, it has to translate part of itself into a lower-dimensional form that can function in three dimensions (or four, counting time as a dimension).

Using my earlier metaphor of higher-order realms and beings

existing "up slope" from us on the top of a hill, incarnation might be seen very simplistically as the soul running down hill to become part of the earth and generating kinetic energy and momentum as it does so. Where does that added energy go to?

Part of it at least becomes our empersonal spirit; it turns into self-light. This does not happen just once. Incarnation is an ongoing process, as if the soul is constantly running down hill and therefore constantly generating momentum and kinetic energy. So this self-light is being generated throughout our life.

There's more to it than this; there usually is when dealing with complex systems in interaction with each other, which is what an incarnation is. Though the common, popular idea is that we incarnate into a body, we actually incarnate into a system of interacting elements, of which the body is one, and the process of integrating these elements together in coherency and wholeness both uses and generates subtle energies that become part of our personal subtle energy field.

A full practice of understanding and attuning to self and to the processes of incarnation from which our everyday self emerges is what Incarnational Spirituality is about. Here is a very simple exercise that I use in some of my classes which can give a flavor of part of the practice at least. I call it the "Three Stars" exercise.

Imagine a spiritual star at the center of the earth. It's a green star radiant with the power of planetary life. Imagine the light from this star rising up through the earth, surrounding you, bathing and nurturing the cells of your body and forming a chalice around you.

Imagine a spiritual star within the sun in the sky. It's a golden star radiant with the power of cosmic life. Imagine the light from this star descending from the heavens and pouring into the chalice of earthlight that surrounds you and fills your cells.

Where the green and golden lights of these two stars

meet in you, a new star emerges, a radiant star of Self-Light, born of the blending of the individual and the universal, the planetary and the cosmic, the physical and the spiritual. This Self-Light surrounds you and fills you, radiating back down deep into the earth and out into space, connecting with the star below you and the star above you. You are a Chalice of Self-Light within a pillar of spiritual energy rising from the earth and descending from the cosmos.

Take a moment to feel the star of this Self-Light within and around you. It is your connection to the earth, your connection to the cosmos, your connection to your own unique and radiant Self. Take a deep breath, drawing this Light into and throughout your body; breathe out, sending this Light out into your world. Filled with this Light of Self, attuned to heaven and earth, go about your day as a star of blessing.

When doing this exercise, you can elaborate it by taking time to give more focused attention to each of the three stars. What does the star of the earth feel like? It symbolizes the presence and Light of Gaia. What do you feel within you or around you in your own personal subtle field when you think of this planetary star and attune to it? Likewise, what is your experience attuning to the cosmic Star? And most importantly, what do you experience as you attune to the generative, radiant star within your own incarnation, within yourself? What happens in your personal subtle energy field as you attune to this inner star of Self-Light, the star of your empersonal spirit?

Attuning to your body and its cells, the body elemental, your personal energy field or aura, and the Light of your own incarnate Self are some of the ways you can begin your engagement with the subtle worlds. In this process, you are gaining familiarity with and influence within the most intimate and vital of these subtle worlds. This is the one that surrounds you and shapes all other contacts you may make.

Field Notes Eight: Soul

There is one aspect of attuning to self that stands out, so I wished to make it the subject of its own set of Field Notes. Indeed, if this is the only subtle contact that you make, it is really sufficient. Nothing else is needed.

This is contact with your own soul.

There are many concepts in the different religions and philosophies of the world about what the soul is, so I want to approach this phenomenologically. What I call the "soul" is something that I first experienced and then later named. Whether I have named this phenomenon correctly depends in part on your beliefs. At the time of that first experience, I had no name for it.

I was living in Morocco at the time. My father was a field agent working for Army Intelligence on counterespionage assignments in the Mediterranean; my mother was a registered nurse working at the hospital on the air force base of Nouasseur where we were living. The closest large city, about twenty miles away, was Casablanca, which is where we would go on shopping trips. One morning in 1952—I was seven at the time—we were en route on such a trip, and I was in the back seat of my parents' car. I was looking out the window watching some Arab women cleaning clothes in an irrigation canal that ran beside the road, using the time-honored method of dipping them in the water and then beating them against stones. To one side of the road was a large billboard advertising an orange soda drink.

I remember feeling a sudden rush of energy and a pressure within me as if I were a balloon swelling up as it was inflated with air. The next thing I knew I was floating in the air above the car, looking down and able to see through the roof as if I were Superman and had X-ray vision. I could clearly see Dad driving and Mom seated next to him, and I could see my own body sitting in the back seat. I could also see the Arab women in the irrigation ditch beside the road as we passed them.

At that point I was surrounded with Light, in which nothing was visible, and I had a sensation of moving at high speed. At intervals, the Light would fade, like clouds parting, and I would see something, sometimes people or just their faces, sometimes glimpses of landscapes, but mostly I was enveloped in Light.

I had no sense of the passage of time. This strange journey could have lasted any duration. It was as if time had ceased to exist for me. But at one point, the Light opened up, and I saw a landscape open before me. I call it a "landscape," but in truth, I'm not sure what it was other than a vast area filled with Light and geometric forms and patterns and beings. What was most powerful about it, though, was a sense of being home. I felt like an amnesiac who had suddenly recovered his memory and now knew who he was. I remember saying so, out loud, "I remember! I remember! I know who I am!" as I stood in this place. I remembered being an eternal being, someone who had existed long before becoming David Spangler. I was in state of consciousness that was utterly familiar but totally different from anything I had experienced when I was David Spangler. I felt fully myself yet fully one with everything around me.

I knew without question that I was experiencing my soul.

There was more to the experience that followed on from this that I find difficult to describe in words, so I won't try, but at some point the experience went in the other direction. In the detached state I was in, I watched the process by which my soul took incarnation on the earth as David Spangler. The memory of what I saw is what I used some fifty years later to begin my research into the nature and process of incarnation that has resulted in what I call Incarnational Spirituality.

The thought of coming to earth filled me with great joy, and the closer I got to the incarnate realms, the more intense the joy and love became. At one point I looked upon the planet as if from space, seeing what astronauts saw nearly two decades later. Then I heard my name being spoken: "David Spangler!" and I was back in my body, looking around. Out the window of the car I saw the same Arab women still beating their clothes against the rocks, and I saw the same billboard advertising the Nehi orange soda drink. Virtually no physical time had passed while I was away on this strange journey.

As I sat in the backseat of the car, I knew exactly what had happened. I remembered it all very clearly (and still do, nearly sixty years later). And the consciousness I opened into, where I felt at home and remembered who I was, is what I called then and still think of now as my "soul."

The soul, to me, is the ultimate origin point for each of our incarnations (you will note that I take reincarnation for granted and always have, particularly since that experience when I was seven). It is who we actually are, a hyperdimensional consciousness existing in what I think of as the "soul levels" of the higher-order worlds.

By its very nature, the soul generally cannot take full incarnation in the physical world. There is too much of it, so to speak, and it is too differently configured as a higher dimensional being and consciousness, to fit into this three-dimensional space. What does incarnate, however, is a part of the soul that organizes itself specifically for taking the incarnational journey into the earth. I think of it as a *fractal* of the soul.

This is hard to describe—I think it really requires some form of hyperdimensional mathematics—but in analogy I think of it this way. Let us say I want to write a novel. I have a seed idea for a plot and for some characters and I want to develop that seed into a book. Part of my mind begins to organize the ideas I have and in time I begin to actually write them down and form them into a narrative. But there are many other parts of my consciousness and of who I am that don't take direct part in this project. I'm a father, a husband, a lover of games, a teacher, and a writer of non-fiction books as well; each of those parts of me contains a great deal of information and experience relevant to its focus. As a father I have a particular awareness that is different from what's in my mind as a husband or as a teacher. I don't try to bring everything I know and think into every role. So it is with my novel. If I add to my narrative all my thoughts about raising my kids or about my life with my wife or what I want to offer my students, the book will become impossibly large, the story will be lost in a mass of detail, and no one will want to buy my novel.

So I have part of my mind that is dedicated to organizing and creating the novel and when I am writing, I bring that part into focus. I put on my "novel writer's cap," so to speak.

We are all familiar with this process, and we also know that in spite of all these different roles, we still are each a whole person. Some part of me, the holistic part or the core part, participates in everything I do. I'm not literally a different person with my kids than with my wife or my students.

When we incarnate, it's as if the soul is writing the story of a life. Not all parts of the soul are engaged in this project, but the part that is I call the "incarnational soul," that is to say, the part of the soul that is configured and focused to be the organizational core of a three-dimensional experience of life. More familiarly, this is what most people, I think, call the "High Self," the overtly spiritual and subtle part of us. And this incarnational soul forms the matrix from which the personality emerges in collaboration with influences and energies from the world around us.

When I sit down to write my novel, I am in that moment separate from all the other "David Spanglers" and their respective roles, such as "David the Father" or "David the Husband." But I am simultaneously united with them through the person and presence of being simply David Spangler. When we incarnate, we separate from the Soul in a manner of speaking, just as my writer's consciousness separates through the mechanism of its concentration and focus from other parts of my life, but we remain one with it at all times as well, just as I remain the same David Spangler that performs all the tasks and lives out all the roles of my life. So in one sense when we incarnate, we don't "go" anywhere at all; we are still the soul we have always been and we are still essentially part of the higher-order worlds; but in another sense, we go on a very different journey indeed into a mode of consciousness and awareness that is unique to the physical dimension and to this world.

Why does this matter?

When I began working with John, he made it very clear that working with him was not a substitute for working with my own soul, for the soul is where each of us touches the deep wellsprings of our beingness and the innate sacredness that each of us carries. Subtle beings can love us and teach us about loving, for instance, but they cannot actually enable us to *be* love. Our souls can. Subtle beings can make clear to us the sacredness that pervades all creation, but they cannot actually enable us to experience and to be that sacredness. Our souls can.

I think of it as a vertical and horizontal partnership. The subtle worlds for me, although most of them are energetically "up slope" from where I am, still exist in a "horizontal" relationship to me. They are "out there," so to speak; my soul is "in here." It is the truly "higher" or more spacious part of me, the vertical part of me that connects me not only to this earth but to the cosmos and to all life and consciousness everywhere.

The soul lives in a subtle realm, a higher-order, hyperdimensional realm, but it is not itself a subtle realm as far as we're concerned, if that makes sense. It's basically the same as saying that I live in Seattle but I am not myself Seattle. If I want to discover who I am and tap my innate potentials of being, going to Seattle is not going to accomplish that. I need to go inward to myself.

In my life and work, contact with my soul informs and shapes my work and contact with the subtle worlds (and with the incarnate world, too, for that matter). If the reason I want to contact the subtle worlds is to receive guidance or find a source of wisdom, then my soul is the better place to go. I am in effect consulting with myself, and this avoids issues of dependency on outside sources or for that matter, fears of deception or manipulation. My soul cannot deceive me, though I can certainly deceive myself or misinterpret what my soul is saying.

The soul lives, breathes, and embodies love. It is rooted in the Sacred and from that ultimate and universal source draws forth love the way we draw sustenance from the earth and oxygen from the air. One consequence of this is that every incarnation begins as an act of love. The soul loves the world and gives itself to function in a reduced state, sacrificing the fullness of its being to be part of the physical dimension, because of this love. There may be other, more specific reasons why a soul seeks incarnation, but behind them all is love. I often tell my classes that we as human beings so love the world that we have given ourselves to be part of it that the world may be better than it was because of us. It is an affirmation of our incarnations and their value.

As I describe later in these Field Notes, an incarnation is a story told in three acts. The first act is in the transitional realms as the soul, in a more focused and compressed seed form as the "incarnate soul" gathers what it needs and prepares for the incarnation. This is the pre-incarnational stage. This is followed by birth and the physical life, which is the second act. During this act, something new emerges around the seed of the personality—the incarnate self—which I might think of as the fruit of that incarnation. The third act begins with physical death and might be seen as the harvesting of that fruit and the reintegration of the personality and the incarnate soul with the soul itself. It's the transition from having been a three-dimensional consciousness into being a hyperdimensional one again. This transition takes place in the Post-Mortem Realms.

The impulse for incarnation that sets these three acts into motion ultimately comes from the soul and its love, but a specific incarnation may, for a variety of reasons, begin elsewhere. To return to the analogy of writing my novel, I may find as I get into it the narrative that it isn't developing as well as I'd hoped. Maybe the main character isn't as good as I thought he or she would be, but a secondary character has come to fore and that person's story is more interesting. So I may abandon that book project for the moment and begin another one that, in a way, stems off from it and emerges from the story I thought I was going to write.

In an analogous fashion, sometimes an incarnation simply doesn't work out as the soul had hoped, but the desire behind it (like my desire to write a novel) is still strong. After physical death, the individuality within the incarnate soul doesn't move back into the higher-order worlds but reincarnates from whatever level it has reached when that decision is made. The karma or ties of the individual to the earthly realm may not let him or her move back into the higher-order realms and union with the soul. Yet even though such a "secondary incarnation" doesn't directly originate with the soul, it's still following through on the original impulse that was born in love—not karma, not obligation, not in the need to learn lessons, but in love and a desire to serve. I find this important to understand for it speaks to our true value and our deepest calling, as well as to our innate capacity for love, a capacity that truly flowers within us when we connect and commune with our soul.

It may seem that the soul is so wonderful and offers so much that it should be our only focus and we should forget the subtle worlds, or for that matter, give it a priority over anything we do in the incarnate realms. But this would be as much a mistake as not seeking out your soul at all. I don't start writing a novel in order to sit at the computer and daydream of something else. We all incarnate because we wish, as souls, to be in this particular kind of realm for a whole variety of reasons, none of which involve wishing we were somewhere else and trying to escape. We are here to learn, to serve, to build, to evolve, to give, to work through challenges, and to be a presence of love. We can do none of those things if we only focus inward and ignore or shortchange our relationships and engagement with an outer world that includes both physical and non-physical dimensions.

I view the subtle realms and my colleagues and allies within them as partners in various tasks and projects, just as I do with my physical friends and family. For those partnerships to exist and flourish, I need to seek them out. I need to co-create them. I need to engage with the world.

But my soul is not my partner in the same way. It is an integral part of me, part of the whole system of my incarnation. The value that others such as my family, friends and colleagues offer comes from the fact that they are different from me. That difference is important for it makes co-creation and the emergence of new ideas and perspectives possible. Others offer me the power and richness that comes from relationships.

My soul, however, *is* me. It is different, yes, but not in the same way that my wife is different from me or a nature spirit is different from me, or John was. I seek partnership with others; I seek oneness with my soul. And I want to bring the richness, grace and lovingness of my soul's energy and presence to those partnerships.

My quest for engagement with the subtle worlds is a quest for co-creative and collaborative partnerships and alliances. My quest for my soul is for wholeness.

I can get perfectly good advice from my wife or from various friends (both incarnate and not), and I seek their counsel and wisdom often. But in the final analysis, I have to depend on my own inner wisdom and decision-making to guide my life, and for that, I want to expand my perspectives into the larger vision and presence that my soul can offer.

But for all the love and wisdom that it has, for all the spiritual energy and power it can offer, my soul cannot offer me a chance to be co-creative and participatory; it cannot offer me the opportunity to encounter differences, to engage with others, to be part of a larger whole, and to make the world a better place.

Jesus asked what it benefited a person to gain the world but lose his or her soul, but in an interesting and seemingly paradoxical way, this can be reversed and we can ask what it benefits a person to gain his or her soul but lose the world. It is not an either/or proposition. It is a partnership, as so many things are in life (particularly in spiritual life), and both soul and world are needed. The soul may *be* love, but part of being is doing, so this could be stated as accurately that the soul *does* love. The value and importance of the earth is that it's a place where the soul, through us, can do that doing.

I cannot tell you how to contact your own soul. That is up to you. People do it in many different ways. In my own case, my soul burst into my earthly consciousness when I was seven years old in what was in some ways a classical mystical experience. In effect, my soul introduced itself to its physical counterpart and extension (me) saying, "I am who you are, and you are also who I am."

But since then there are things I do to keep that contact fresh. Taking time each day to quietly attune to its presence is important, if only by thinking about, asking "what might my soul do in this instance, " and then listening quietly for a response. I seek out things that will remind me of my soul or that inspire me with a sense of my soul; these might be works of art, poetry, the iconic beauty of the sunset, reading spiritual literature, or something other that I find puts me in mind and heart of my soul.

Since the soul is a presence of love, perhaps the most effective form of communion is to do acts of loving, of compassion, and of kindness. How can you help another? How can you bring wholeness and healing into a situation? What can you do from where you are, with what you have available within and around you, and as who you are right now to make your world, in the form of your immediate environment and the things and creatures and people within it, a better place?

In short, act *as* your soul and you will find in time you become your soul.

Field Notes Nine:
Tidal Pools

The terms "non-physical worlds" and "subtle realms" are accurate as far as they go, but they cover such a wide range of phenomena as to be practically useless when it comes to distinguishing or understanding the various realms and the beings within them. It's a bit like using the term "ocean" to describe the watery part of our planet. Do we mean the deep ocean where creatures exist that never see the light of day and perish if brought to the surface of the water or close to it? Do we mean the relatively more shallow waters over the continental shelves? Do we mean the seashore where ocean waves roll ashore on sandy beaches? All of it is surely the "ocean," but obviously there are distinct regions where different conditions exist and particular kinds of animals and plants can live.

In an earlier set of Field Notes, I wrote about the personal subtle field that surrounds each of us and which is an emanation of our own bodies, minds, feelings, spirit, and incarnational processes. This field has a boundary that differentiates it from the larger subtle environment that is part of the earth and the vast realms beyond. This boundary is permeable and elastic, able to expand and contract, but it's still there; the health, integrity and sovereignty of our incarnation depend on it.

If the larger expanse of the non-physical dimensions is the "ocean" and our unique, individual life, personality and body form the "land," then our personal subtle energy field—our aura—is like the beach and the seashore, the place where the two meet and intermingle.

In a similar way, the physical planet itself has its own "personal" subtle energy field that it generates in much the same way that we generate our own on an individual level. I've called this the subtle fields of the incarnate realms. We could think of it as Gaia's aura. The energies of the transitional and higher-order realms sweep into and out of this planetary aura in a tidal fashion, much like the waves of the ocean move onto and away from the beach in the rhythm of the tides.

The subtle fields that make up this planetary aura are the one's closest energetically to human consciousness and to the physical plane. All things being equal, these fields are the easiest to discern and attune to. They are where, for instance, we feel the atmosphere of a room or area. To return momentarily to the metaphor of the hill slope, these fields are only a step or two up the hill.

The analogy with the seashore is useful in thinking about these "nearby" subtle fields. When I visit the beach, I can find items that fell into the ocean from the land, perhaps during a storm, and have now been washed up on the sand. These can be logs and even pieces of lumber, leaves from trees, bottles, and the like. This is analogous to how bits of our own energetic selves—energies generated by thoughts and feelings, usually—split off from us and become part of the general subtle atmosphere that fills the environment. And just as flotsam and jetsam washed up on a beach could come from anywhere along the ocean, sometimes swept thousands of miles on ocean currents, so these energetic bits that "wash up" into our immediate subtle environment could come from people or events many miles away.

The same is true for the psychic debris that we may generate. Our anger, hatred or fear, if radiated strongly enough, could in fact produce an equivalent energy that ends up affecting and influencing someone hundreds or thousands of miles away. However, this same phenomenon works to our advantage when performing subtle activism. A clearly and powerfully broadcast thought of love, compassion, peace, and healing can travel widely in the energetic ocean of the earth's subtle aura and affect many people in positive ways far beyond our knowledge or the reach of our physical resources.

For twenty years, Dr. Brugh Joy and I sponsored and co-hosted a New Year's conference at the Asilomar Conference Center in Monterey, California. This is a beautiful facility, located right on the beach overlooking Monterey Bay and the Pacific Ocean. Whenever the conference wasn't in session, my family and I would go down to the beach and walk and play in the water. We particularly enjoyed exploring the tidal pools. Formed in depressions in the rocks along the seashore, these were pools of sea water left behind when the tide went out. They contained small creatures such as sea anemones, starfish, crabs, and sea slugs that normally lived in ocean but now were living in these small pools surrounded by the land. Creatures like these might otherwise be hard to see in the ocean itself, but we could walk right up to a tidal pool and see what treasures the ocean had temporarily left behind. The tidal pools were accessible to ourselves as inhabitants of the land.

There are "tidal pools" of subtle energy and life as well. They are created where the activity of human beings interacting with the subtle energies of the incarnate realms—the aura of the planet—meets the tides and waves of life and consciousness sweeping in through the transitional realms from the higher-order worlds beyond. These metaphysical "tidal pools" form some of the most accessible areas for feeling into the non-physical worlds and engaging with subtle beings.

What are these tidal pools?

They are the familiar artifacts we produce in our lives, ranging from buildings we inhabit to objects we create. Where human thought and creativity interacts with matter, an energetic "tidal pool" may come into being as well. I described this process with regard to my sofa in an earlier set of Field Notes. Just as depressions in rocks can create the environment for a tidal pool to form at a seashore, so the impact of human mental, emotional, and spiritual activity creates a configuration within subtle matter that can allow a field of energy to form separate from the currents and tides of subtle energies flowing through the world. This field may then be an energy environment within which a subtle being can live or to which it can connect. The intensity and quality of that field affects the kind of being that can or might associate with it, if in fact any being does.

I don't want to get into the theory and metaphysics of all this, but I do want to offer some examples of what I mean. Hopefully, these will provide suggestions of ways to practice engagement with subtle energies and beings.

Go to a room in your house. Sit quietly at first and feel the subtle energy—the "atmosphere" or mood—within this room. Then get up and move about the room, keeping your attention focused on sensing the subtle field through which you're moving. What is the felt sense of this room for you? What do you feel in your body? When you feel you have a sense of this, get up and go to another room. What is the subtle energy in that room? Does it feel different?

Repeat this through all the rooms where you live. If you have a walk-in closet, even try that space out. Observe the differences you feel in each room.

When we enclose a space with walls, we create an energetic "tidal pool" in the space within those walls. The walls, after all, are not just physical; they have a subtle counterpart as well, which can be augmented by your intent; you can reinforce the subtle walls by directing energy into them through your will. In a new house, this space will be relatively unconditioned, but after a person has lived in it for a while and made use of the space, it begins to take on character and an atmosphere. The energy a person puts into the space by the nature of his or her thoughts, feelings and activities begins to build up, becoming a presence within the room.

Sometimes this energy can be intensified within a room around a particular piece of furniture or a special object. We have a large room downstairs that has seen many uses over the years. Initially, it was a family room. Then later I made it my home office. Still later, it served as a classroom when I gave workshops in my home. Then as we had more children and they got older, we divided the space and turned it into two bedrooms.

At one point in this process, I used part of the space as a sanctuary where I did much of my inner work. It had a simple altar in it on which I would light a candle and sometimes burn some incense while meditating. Eventually, I moved my working space elsewhere in the house as we needed to use the larger room for something else, but for months afterwards, I could go into that room and feel the energy still concentrated where the altar had been. In effect, the altar had created a small energetic tidal pool of its own.

An exercise I sometimes give people in my classes to illustrate this phenomenon is to make an altar in a room where they live. It doesn't have to be elaborate. What it looks like and what's on it really doesn't matter; what counts is the energy that is focused upon it and the quality and consistency of that energy. I ask them to do something on or around the altar everyday that the class lasts; it could be lighting a candle, putting a vase of fresh flowers, saying a prayer. More important than any specific action are the attention and energy the person gives to what he or she does, as well as to the altar. Then I ask them to observe how the energy in the room changes having the altar there, as well as to observe the energy directly around the altar.

I've yet to have a class in which people did not experience a change of energy with this exercise. Likewise, I've yet to have a class in which, when I ask people to walk through their home attuning to the different rooms, they fail to sense and feel how the subtle energy changes from room to room. This kind of subtle perception is fairly simple and grows out of sensitivities that most of us use every day in assessing places, situations, and people. Energetic tidal pools are everywhere and they're comparatively easy to feel into.

Here's another exercise. Pick a piece of furniture in your house—a sofa, a chair, a table, it doesn't matter— and hold your hands about three or four inches above its surface. Now move your hands around, keeping that distance between them and the piece of furniture. Do you feel anything? Whether you do or not, after a couple of minutes, go to a different piece of furniture and do the same thing? Do you feel anything now? Does it feel different from the first time? Go to a third piece of furniture and repeat.

I use furniture here only because chairs, sofas, tables, and the like are large enough to move your hands around over them comfortably, and they provide more space in which to feel their subtle energy. But you could do this same exercise with any object or set of objects. At first you may not feel anything, but if you practice, chances are you will. I can't guarantee it, of course, for people are different. It's one reason I feel this kind of thing has to be taught in person as a kind of apprenticeship rather than through a book. But in my experience, a majority of people will in fact discern energetic differences between the different pieces of furniture or between different objects when they do this.

There is a form of psychic perception, called *psychometry*, in which a person can hold an object, tune into its subtle field and "read" from it all kinds of information. I had a friend some years ago who was able to do this quite skillfully and easily. She often was hired to go on archeological expeditions to psychometrize things the archeologists would dig up and give them information about what it was and the culture it came from.

But in this exercise, I'm not asking you to do this. The purpose here is much more modest and simple, which is to become aware of the subtle energies of the incarnate field that surround us all the time and to experience how these energies can collect into metaphysical "tidal pools" around objects and places. As you begin to have a feeling of this energy, it opens a door to sensing and perceiving the beings who work or live in these tidal pools.

What I've described so far is like finding the tidal pools and seeing the water in them. That's a start. But if you probe a bit deeper, you will find the metaphysical equivalent of anemones, starfish, and crabs—and at times beings much more powerful than that.

Once I was walking from my bedroom into the bathroom when I felt a strong tug on my consciousness. It's a bit like having someone grab your sleeve or your shirttail and give it a pull, only it happens energetically. This has happened many times over the years, and when it does, I pause and shift my attention to the subtle energy field around me.

In this case, I was truly surprised to find a group of small beings extending themselves somewhat from the wall of the bedroom. They did not look like much more than blobs with eyes to me, like giant single celled organisms, but as I watched, a facsimile of a human face appeared in many of them. They spoke in unison, like a choir, and they all said, "Go outside, David! Go outside!"

I asked who and what they were and why I should go outside. They said that they were beings who lived in the walls of buildings and acted as intermediaries in the flow of subtle energy between the interior of the building and the world outside. Their task was to make the energetic walls of a building, like my house, more permeable and to regulate the energetic relationship between, in this case, the house and the surrounding environment. As to why they wanted me to be outside, they said they could feel that my energy was becoming too housebound (I have a tendency to stay indoors a lot when I'm working on a project and to forget to go out). There were beings outside, they said, in the trees and bushes mainly, who had told them they wanted to "charge up" my energy field and I needed to go outside to do that (it's nice to know my backyard cares for me!). So I went outside, and indeed, I felt very much better for having done so.

A biologist friend of mine used to put a bucket in a pond and extract it full of pond water. Then he would just sit and stare at that water, paying close attention to it. One day I asked him about this, and he said, "I'm observing the life that's in this water as it gives me clues about the overall state and health of the pond." He then had me look, and sure enough, there were all kinds of small critters floating and swimming in the water in the bucket (not to mention the microbes, of course; they were not visible without a microscope).

In an analogous way, when I sit here and contemplate the room around me, I'm aware of a host of different kinds of simple non-physical life forms. Just this one room is a whole ecology by itself, much less the whole house. Just as a house is a place that a great many physical creatures other than its human owners call home—insects, bacteria, maybe birds, maybe mice, and other kinds of critters—the same is true in the subtle worlds.

I'm aware, for instance, of what I call the house spirit or the house angel, a being who overlights the house as a whole and all of us as a family who live within it. The idea of house spirits is an ancient one. In our case, it's field of energy enfolds the house and the ground it stands on. We have fir and maple trees near our house, and I can feel their energy as part of the house's energy as well. In this room, I'm aware of the tiny spirits in the walls and ceiling, I'm aware of simple beings who have associated themselves with certain objects in the room and rather more powerful beings who are connected to my altar. As I say, it's a very rich tidal pool.

The point is that you don't have to reach out to vast cosmic or planetary realms of consciousness to make contact with the subtle worlds. The subtle energy field of the planet is all around us all the time, and it is filled with the "tidal pools" that we have created where simple beings of one kind or another can live and be nourished by our energy or perform simple tasks that aid them in the growth of their consciousnesses. The ecology I described for my room is true in principle for any room. Your workplace is a tidal pool as well which may repay your investigation and sympathetic attunement.

Most of us ignore these tidal pools, being unaware of them, and we are ignored for the most part in turn by the beings within them. Although I call them simple beings who live at the interface between the planetary energy field and the ocean of Light and energy found in the transitional and higher-order worlds, they can still be quite powerful as allies. If I send them love and appreciation as fellow life forms, they will respond. Their love and appreciative energy coming back can totally change the atmosphere in a room, filling it with blessing.

In effect, when we notice them and acknowledge them (even by so simple an act as saying "Hi!" to a room when we enter it and filling it with a wave of our love), they will notice us in return; their consciousness is heightened by the energy we send them and a relationship begins to build. This relationship in turn can be hugely supportive and empowering, particularly when it comes to time to extend your consciousness outward into the more distant subtle worlds—that is, to go upslope—and their help can be invaluable as well when performing subtle activism.

When it comes to engaging with subtle worlds, wading in the tidal pools is a good place to start.

Field Notes Ten:
Making a Difference

In the Beginning, God created the universe by making a difference.

If I were writing my own creation story, that's how I would start it. Or as the French would say (though admittedly in another context altogether), *Vive La Différence!*

In this set of Field Notes, I want to wax philosophical for a moment. I promise to be brief, not to get terribly metaphysical or complex, and to tie these thoughts in to our theme of engaging with the subtle worlds. And in fact, understanding differences and how to work with them is a major component of working with the non-physical realms.

The key fact about difference is that it generates activity; among other things, it creates a flow. Think of how air flows from warmer regions to cooler regions or from areas of higher pressure to areas of lower pressure. It's this differential that is responsible for generating winds and creating our weather.

Throughout these Field Notes, I've been talking about energy differentials; I've talked about consciousness moving "upslope" and "down slope," about the energy difference between the higher-order worlds and the incarnate, physical realms. It's these differences that are partly responsible for the flow of energy and life through the planetary system.

For that matter, the difference in energy between you as an embodied physical person and your own soul generates a vital circulation of spiritual energy all on its own, quite apart from anything you consciously invoke from higher levels of being. This circulation is, in fact, one of the important reasons why incarnation takes place.

In some respects, it may be the main reason.

I wasn't kidding when I said I would begin my creation story by emphasizing the making of a difference—the creation of differentials—as the Sacred's primary creative act. In many existing creation stories, we have God as the unknowable, indefinable, immeasurable, unmanifest with creation as knowable, definable, measureable, and manifest. This is a profound difference, and this difference sets up the primal generative flow—the "Breath of God"—that activates and stimulates all life and sets the cosmos into motion. Nor does this flow only move in one direction; it is a circulation moving from the unmanifest to the manifest and back again.

It is certainly a legitimate question to ask why the planetary system is arranged and organized as it is with a physical realm that appears on the surface so limited and constricted paired with a very different hyperdimensional realm that is so much more spacious and energetic, linked by a series of transitional realms. But the reason is precisely that this kind of differential is highly generative; it's a kind of engine of spiritual energy. In part the transitional realms themselves are brought into being—and provide an environment in which lifeforms can evolve and grow and give service—by the flow and circulation of energy produced by this differential. And what makes that possible is that both extremes are held in tension and relationship by the consciousness and energy field of the World Soul.

In this context, incarnation—the movement of consciousness from the higher-order worlds into the three-dimensional world and back again—is a manifestation and an implementation of this circulation. Incarnation is not so much a soul getting inside a body as it is a hyperdimensional consciousness and a three-dimensional consciousness (soul and bodymind or personality) paired as part of a miniature system that like the planet itself generates and circulates spiritual energies because of the differences between these two parts. And this facilitates the circulation of higher-order energies and incarnate energies as well. In effect, the process of incarnation is part of what holds the world together energetically.

Where energy flows, consciousness is stimulated and

empowered; if energy gets blocked, stagnation and a diminishment of life and power can occur. Part of the challenge of the world right now is that energy is blocked within the activity of humanity—in part due to the level of violence and divisiveness we express—and in the relationship of humanity to the natural world. We turn differences, which could be creative and energizing between us, into reasons for conflict, largely because we still fear what is different; or in the case of nature, we use our difference from the rest of the natural world as an excuse not to be stewards and partners but to dominate and exploit. We still have many lessons to learn about differences.

I have said several times in these Field Notes that there is a major effort within the higher-order and transitional realms to heal the obstructions humanity is creating and re-establish a co-creative partnership in love and consciousness between the different elements of the planetary system. To be part of that effort—to join in partnership with subtle beings to use our differences to enhance the circulation of spirit for the healing and transformation of the world—is for me the major reason for attempting to engage with the non-physical worlds. It's not to get guidance or to be told what to do; it's not to be taken care of by some heavenly parents; it's not to satisfy our curiosity or to appear special in the eyes of others. It's to work, and work hard, at restoring wholeness to the earth system in alliance and partnership with beings whom we've either ignored or misunderstood for far too long.

There is another reason why an understanding of difference and flow is important.

In the previous set of Field Notes, when I was describing the exercises with the metaphysical "tidal pools," you may remember I suggested you walk about or you move your hands around in order to sense the subtle fields and energies.

It's been my experience that if I just stand still and try to tune in to the subtle worlds, it's much harder to do. It's harder to pick up on a static field of energy. It's much easier if it's moving or if I am, usually the latter. What I'm really sensing most of the time is an energy differential. If I'm in a room, I get a better sense of its energetic "tidal pool" if I sense into it from one place in the room, then change and sense into it from a different spot and also pay attention to whatever differences I feel by moving about.

In my experience, I often find it easier to contact a subtle being if I'm on a walk than if I'm just standing or sitting still. And if I am sitting, I find I begin to sway, like seaweed in a current. I move my hands along my thighs. Some part of me is in motion and needs to be; if I become perfectly still, I often lose the contact.

Of course, there are different kinds of movement, too. My movement when I'm in contact with an inner being is not random or jerky or simple restlessness. It's always rhythmic, just as a circulation is rhythmic. I confess I don't fully understand the mechanism of this, I just know what works and what I have experienced. And given the importance of making a difference and honoring and working with differentials, I imagine this movement is yet another manifestation of that same principle.

Field Notes Eleven:
Pit Crew

In the folk tales of many cultures, there are legends of creatures who live in the sea, such as mermaids and selkies, who have the power, usually by setting aside their native form, to walk the land among human beings. In an analogous way, there are many non-physical beings who normally live in the higher-order worlds but have the ability to function in the transitional realms and even in the subtle fields of the physical. I have mentioned some of them who may be found in the "tidal pools" of our artifacts and our homes.

There is one group of such beings, though, who are particularly close to each of us, able to adjust their energy when needed, come "down slope" and move into our immediate subtle environment to give help. In the process of developing our capacity to engage with the subtle worlds, these beings are the closest and easiest to contact outside of our own personal energy fields and the tidal pools that we create.

Who are they?

Basically they are those beings who have a particular connection and affinity with you and are able through both desire and training to be in a position to help you as much as possible in your incarnation. Because of their resonance with you, they can attune their own consciousnesses to yours in a way that allows them access to your energy fields. This resonance and familiarity may have different sources. They may have known you and been close to you in other lives. In this life, they may have chosen to stay behind in the higher-order and transitional realms in order to be a potential partner for you as you took up physical embodiment. They may be beings who have a shared interest or some other commonality of energy. Their basic intent where you are concerned is that your incarnation is a success and fulfills the goals you set for yourself when you decided to enter the physical world. They are, in effect, the equivalent of an inner family.

Metaphorically, if your life is driving on a race track (and it may feel that way sometimes), they are the beings who act as your "pit crew," giving you aid and assistance if they can and rooting for you as you circle around. This doesn't mean, by the way, that they are hovering around you all the time or are even aware of you all the time, though their attunement to you is such that they will most likely know if you have need of them. They have their own lives and affairs as well to occupy their attention. But like family or close friends, they are the ones who are most attuned to you and familiar with you. In a time of need, they would most likely be the first responders.

Using a different analogy, if you are the astronaut in the space shuttle or landing on the moon, your Pit Crew are among those who work to make this possible. They are not simply friends and allies on the inner, though they are that, too; they are an integral part of your incarnation seen as a whole system or project, just as the technicians in NASA are part of the mission of putting a person on the moon, even though they're not the ones in the space suits venturing beyond the planet.

Who is in your Pit Crew is unique to you. They are most likely human beings living and working in the subtle realms, but they can be non-human beings as well. By this I don't mean extraterrestrials, but they could be nature spirits with whom you have formed an affinity or a specific angelic being, who in this instance could well be considered a "guardian angel." Indeed, there is a class of being whom we'll discuss later who might be called "human elementals," or even "angels of the human species," and such a being may well be an integral part of your Pit Crew. If you have had shamanic experiences and attracted an "animal power" or an ally from the plant kingdom, then that being might remain attuned to you and be part of your Pit Crew as well.

It is not necessarily automatic that a close friend or a family member in this life, such as a parent or sibling, who has died will be part of your Pit Crew. In my own experience and understanding, it's rare for anyone newly dead and new to the Post-Mortem Realms to be a part of a Pit Crew because they lack the experience for the task and are more than likely involved with finding their own equilibrium and place in their new life in the subtle realms.

This does not mean that such a person could not "drop in" on you now and again in a helpful way. Both of my parents are deceased and living on the inner, and neither is part of my Pit Crew, though they do appear now and again to say hello, to let me know they're all right and to see how I'm doing. However, it is quite possible that a more remote ancestor could be part of your Pit Crew.

Sometimes a Pit Crew member isn't anyone you have known before on any level but is "assigned" to you because of a particular task you have agreed to perform on earth. Or it could be a teacher or mentor you have on the inner who is concerned about your progress.

Some Pit Crew members will be closer to you and more attentive to you than others, but as I say, none of them is with you all the time, 24/7. They are not a crowd of invisible beings who go with you every place you go, like the "network" in the Verizon television commercials. But in a sense you are with them all the time. You are held in their fields so that if there is a need or you call to them, there is an alert that signals their attention and consciousness so that they can be with you in a more specific and immediate fashion, if that is appropriate and possible in that moment. In short, you are on speed dial with them!

The function of the Pit Crew and the way it relates to you can vary from person to person. In most cases, their role is not to give you messages or provide you with guidance, though there can be circumstances when they may do that; they are not there to take over your life or to interfere. But they do link their energy with yours and will seek to form a collaborative field with you that enhances your own thinking and feeling.

As I understand it, the core of the Pit Crew is there from birth onwards. It is formed around you prior to your coming into incarnation. Some of its members may have been instrumental in helping with your incarnational process and the transition from the non-physical to the physical realm. At the same time, there are those who come into your Pit Crew at different times in your life, who may be in it for a period of time, and then may leave, their contribution essentially finished.

Certainly, you can invite a non-physical being to join your Pit Crew if you feel an affinity with it; whether and how that being responds is another matter, but the invitation counts. Membership in a Pit Crew can get fuzzy along the edges, like a party in which a core of people are there from the beginning and stay through to the end and others come and go throughout the evening. The key element here is not longevity but attunement. What makes a person or being part of your Pit Crew is his, her, or its resonance with your specific incarnational process.

Why is a Pit Crew important in the process of engaging with subtle worlds? Think of yourself as traveling to a big city or a foreign country with which you are unfamiliar. How nice it is if you already have family or friends there who can provide you a loving and supportive base of operations as you learn your way around. Your Pit Crew is made up of exactly those kinds of beings. They can act as a portal or interface with the larger ecology of the inner worlds. Not that you have to always go through them as intermediaries, but it's nice to know they're there.

In a way, John, who was part of my Pit Crew for at least twenty-seven years (he may have been around before he introduced himself to me, and I didn't know it), performed that function for me, at least at first. He was the intermediary between me and the larger ocean of the subtle worlds until I had learned to navigate for myself.

How do you tune into your Pit Crew? Now we're beginning to venture into those areas of technique that are dependent on who you are individually, and in this case, who your Pit Crew is. Not all Pit Crews are created equal and some are larger than others. Some are more active in a person's life, and some pretty much fade into the background, for reasons dictated by the characteristics and purposes of the incarnation itself. Some people quite naturally attune to their Pit Crews while others make different contacts with the subtle worlds, bypassing the Pit Crew altogether. It all depends on what is right and natural for you, and without knowing you, I cannot prejudge that.

Attuning to and establishing a relationship with one or more members of your Pit Crew is a bit like finding and establishing a relationship with a potential spouse. This is a very individual matter. In my own case, members of my Pit Crew made themselves known to me at an early age when I was a child. I did not have to seek them out. Therefore, I don't have a generic technique for doing so that I learned myself. When I teach this part of my classes, I encourage each person to find their own mode of attunement, and I will help in whatever way I can.

However, I have a general suggestion. If you were looking for a spouse, you would first think about what you would want in a life partner and you'd probably form some image of the qualities that such a person would embody. And you would think about the kinds of places where you might meet such a person.

Attuning to a member of your Pit Crew is not so different. Who or what do you think a being would be like who cares for you and seeks to enable you to be a success in your life? Never mind what it might look like. What qualities would it have? What qualities would it bring to you? What would you offer or give such a being in return in the form of love and appreciation?

Then imagine a being that fulfills those qualities present invisibly in your life. The form or shape that you imagine doesn't really matter. Like my son's stuffed toy that became a touch point for a guardian spirit, the imaginal shape you create can simply serve as a touch point for your Pit Crew to engage with your awareness. Practice being aware of them and acknowledging them, using this inner construct as a tool, and chances are that you will find yourself becoming aware of the energy of their presence.

Field Notes Twelve:
The Imaginal

You unlock this door with the key of imagination. Beyond it is another dimension: a dimension of sound, a dimension of sight, a dimension of mind. You're moving into a land of both shadow and substance, of things and ideas. You've just crossed over into...

In the 1960's when Rod Serling wrote and narrated this introduction to his award winning television show, the place you've "crossed over into" was the Twilight Zone. But I could just as easily use this introduction (or any of the others Serling wrote for the program) to introduce a particular subtle realm I call *The Imaginal*.

In most esoteric and psychic traditions, this realm is called *the Astral*, so called because in the Middle Ages those who worked with it clairvoyantly perceived its substance sparkling like the stars and named it "astral" which meant "star-like" in Latin. But I call it the "Imaginal" because, like the Twilight Zone it's a dimension of imagination, or more precisely a realm strongly influenced and shaped by the power of imagination, particularly when backed up by emotion and other subtle energies.

The Imaginal realm is part of the incarnate realms. It might be thought of as a realm of undifferentiated creative substance, possessing no character of its own but therefore able to be molded into anything and given character by the one doing the molding. As such it has many possible uses, particularly in the areas of manifestation and creativity. Using the Astral or Imaginal dimension as a tool in manifestation is a traditional part of esoteric and magical teaching and outside the scope of these Field Notes.

The Imaginal can be a place where our collective imaginations run wild, creating images that then can be picked up and read by someone who is sensitive to the subtle realms. The challenge is that these images may not reflect anything real but just express the fears that are in the collective human unconscious.

Once I was entertaining a friend who lived in Europe but was visiting me in the United States. It was a time of tension between the United States and the Soviet Union. There was concern that a new world war might break out with Soviet forces invading Germany and sweeping westward across Europe. My friend was concerned and asked if I'd tune in and see if I could see from an inner perspective whether war might break out. If so, he would move himself and his family to be out of harm's way.

This kind of prophetic perception is not something I'm particularly good at, though I have had a few successes over the years. But that evening I saw what amounted to a small movie with tanks rolling across the countryside and jet fighters engaged in dog fights over European cities. It certainly looked like war, and I told my friend so.

After he went to bed, however, I began to question what I had been seeing. It had been very vivid but in some ways its very vividness made it suspect to me. Further, for all the sound and fury the images represented, there was a curious lack of energy about them, as if they were hollow with nothing backing them up. I decided to tune in again now that I was alone and see if I saw the same things.

As it turned out, I didn't. There were no signs or images of war at all. I realized then that what I had seen was a "movie" in the Imaginal reams which had been attached to my friend, who was newly arrived from Europe. It obviously represented some strong fears that many Europeans had and was their imagination of something that could happen or that they feared would happen. But there was no reality behind it at all. There would be no war.

I told my friend this when he got up in the morning, and he was much relieved. But he shared with me that as he was going to bed, he'd tuned in as well and had been assured by his intuition and inner contacts that all was well. So in some manner, the playing of that "movie" in his presence helped to discharge the energy of fear it (and he) was carrying.

This kind of movie is not uncommon on the Imaginal realm. If a psychic is not skilled in discernment or has little knowledge of the Imaginal realm, he or she might tune in and see one of these narratives and believe that it's real. I'm convinced that many prophecies that we hear now and again ultimately come from this kind of imaginal experience.

These movies are one variation of a common phenomenon of the Imaginal realm, a phenomenon that's important to consider and understand when it comes to exploring and engaging with the subtle worlds. This is the phenomenon of *thought-forms* and it's what I want to focus upon in this set of Field Notes.

If you think of a chocolate cake, you've created a thought image which has a particular shape. Through the influence of your imagination on your own personal subtle field, it will become part of that field for as long as you think of it. If you invest that image with enough emotional and mental energy, particularly in the form of desire and will, you can propel that image out of your own personal subtle field into the subtle energies of the imaginal realm. At that point it becomes a thought-form. Under the right circumstances, it can detach from you and gain a semi-autonomous existence, assuming it can draw energy from somewhere else to sustain it. If someone else draws that thought-form into their personal subtle field, they may find themselves suddenly and unaccountably thinking of and desiring a chocolate cake.

Most thought-forms are created willy-nilly in moments of intense emotion but lack any consistent or persistent follow through that would "bulk them up" energetically and sustain them in existence. They dissolve fairly quickly and certainly never get beyond the aura of the person who created it. But some become much more long-lasting and can even gain an autonomous existence, assuming some energy source is keeping them active. At that point they can act like a being, seeking to fulfill the objectives for which they were created. They become a kind of non-physical robot, following their programming. And like a robot, they normally have little or no flexibility to change or transform.

Thought-forms can become very complex and powerful, though, particularly when they are born from the imaginations and emotions of large collectives of people. Any religion, for example, can be the source for numerous thought-forms shaped, held and empowered by the faithful. Many such thought-forms can be benign and helpful, but some, particularly when born from emotions of anger, hatred, fear, or aggression, can be toxic and harmful. And as a thought-form becomes more energized and complex, it can begin to act more and more like a being, gaining a certain flexibility of choice and direction. But they are still "robots" at heart.

Many thought-forms existing in the Imaginal originate from the stories we tell in mythology or in novels and movies or other forms of modern popular entertainment. They take shape and continue in existence because people continue to imagine them and give them energy. It *is* possible, for instance, to find Superman or Sherlock Holmes in the Imaginal realms!

As an example of this, my friend R. Ogilvie Crombie, the Scottish gentleman who was the primary contact with the nature spirits at Findhorn, tells of traveling across the island of Mull off the west coast of Scotland. Peter Caddy, one of the founders of Findhorn, was driving, and the two of them were going across a particularly desolate, wind-swept region. Roc, as he was known from his initials, suddenly felt that they had entered a patch of dense, unpleasant negative subtle energies which stayed with them for some miles. They could see no reason for the negativity outwardly, but the psychic atmosphere felt dense nonetheless.

About midway through this area, Roc spotted movement along the ridgeline of a group of hills near the road. As he looked more closely, he saw to his astonishment that it was a group of orcs coming over and down the hillside. They were exactly as described by Tolkien in the *Lord of the Rings* trilogy. Roc realized he was seeing them clairvoyantly and that their presence was due to the negativity in the subtle energies in that area. "These were not real orcs, of course," Roc told me later in describing this experience, "but enough people have now read Tolkien's trilogy that the image of orcs has become part of the inner worlds and can be used like a suit of clothes by inner beings of a negative bent."

This story illustrates that the Imaginal realm is not just the province of human thought. Subtle beings can use it just as well to create forms with which to contact human beings, or simply to make contact with the physical level. In so doing, they can borrow images supplied by human imagination, like browsing through a great costume shop.

For example, there is a thought-form of Jesus held and maintained by the thoughts and devotion of millions of Christian believers. Jesus to them represents a sacred figure to whom they can turn in prayer for guidance and help. A being such as a discarnate human teacher from the higher-order worlds may respond to such prayers or seek to contact a believer but is either unnoticed or rejected because he doesn't fit within that believer's worldview. However, if he "slips into" the Jesus thought-form and uses it as a mode of communication and contact, then the believer may well respond and accept the help that is given. (It should be noted that the "Jesus thought-form" is a template that can be used simultaneously by many inner beings, much as many people might buy and wear a particular mask on Halloween.)

One of my favorite thought-form stories occurred when I was in England and visiting friends in Oxford. C.S. Lewis, the author of the *Narnia Chronicles, The Great Divorce*, and other wonderful books, is buried there in Holy Trinity Churchyard. As a fan of many of his books, I wanted to pay my respects at his grave. I knew full well that he wouldn't be there, but it seemed the thing to do, and the burial ground is a beautiful spot.

When we got to his grave, I stood there looking at it and thought of all the pleasurable moments I had spent reading his books. Suddenly, the man himself appeared standing at the end of his grave. This surprised me greatly. Was C.S. Lewis earthbound, tied to the resting place of his body? As I wondered at this, I felt a lovely blessing coming from this entity. Then it just stood there, staring benignly at me or actually, as I realized in a moment, *through* me. Cranking up my own sensitivity to look more closely and deeply,

I realized that there was no soul force animating this figure and that it was in fact a thought-form of Lewis. It lasted for a moment, then it disappeared.

Apparently, like one of the audioanimatronic robots of famous people one encounters in Disneyland, it had been created — whether by Lewis or not, I couldn't tell, though I doubted it — in order to respond to well-wishers who came to the gravesite. It's single and simple purpose was to give a blessing of love, triggered by the proximity of thoughts of appreciation about Lewis and his writings. In other words, it was programmed to respond to the presence of a fan. It was a very benign and sweet thought-form indeed, and I did feel blessed by it.

The reason I bring up the topic of thought-forms is that anyone exploring the subtle realms is almost certain to run into them from time to time. Sometimes it can be difficult to tell one apart from a real being, particularly if it's well-formed and relatively complex in its behavior or if it's being animated and used like a suit of clothes by a living consciousness. This can be a problem because such "costumes" can be used for deceptive purposes. Discernment is important, and that's an issue I'll discuss in a later set of Field Notes.

In my own experience, most thought-forms have certain tell-tale characteristics. They have a limited repertoire of actions, words, and responses; they may exist for one purpose only which is to transmit a particular energy to a recipient, rather like an inner plane telegram. They can feel robotic or hollow, lacking the spark that a living being has. They may also be very focused in their energy, which can come across as a kind of pushiness or insistence much like you might feel from an aggressive salesperson. There is a lack of caring or concern for anything or anyone other than what fulfills the purpose of the thought-form; in other words, it doesn't care what you think, only that you accept what it thinks. (Of course, there can be people and subtle beings who have that characteristic as well!)

But sometimes if the thought-form is, as I said, complex and well-developed or if it's being used as a costume by another being, these tell-tales may be overridden. If I'm not sure what I'm dealing with. I always insist that I be shown the true nature of whatever is in my field and that it stand in the Light of the Sacred and the Self-Light of my own sovereignty, respecting both. I may call upon my Pit Crew or other allies to help me, and I pay attention to whatever felt sense may be arising in my body concerning this phenomenon.

If after using my best skills of discernment and attunement, I still can't tell, then my rule of thumb is to walk away and leave it alone, or, as John suggested, just say no to it and tell it to go. I have always found that any true being who wants to work with me and has my welfare and partnering as its objective will find a way to communicate clearly who and what it is and its intent, and if it can't, it will come back when it can.

Thought-forms can certainly be used for good, as when I create one to send a blessing to someone, and at times they can mediate energies and intelligences coming from realms unused to dealing with incarnate consciousnesses. But they are double-edged tools and need to be used with care.

Field Notes Thirteen:
The Post-Mortem Realms

Where do we go when we die? That is the question that people have asked through the millennia. It is the journey that each of us will take one day, and obviously we'd like to know the destination.

I have my own perceptions of this, of course. You cannot engage with the subtle worlds without in some manner running into the idea of an afterlife. In a real way, the non-physical realms *are* the afterlife or more appropriately, the continuing of life. However, at this stage of humanity's spiritual evolution, it is the rare individual who jumps directly from the three-dimensional experience and development of the incarnate realms directly into hyperdimensional life within the higher-order worlds. As I have already related in the set of Field Notes on the soul, some time needs to be spent in which an incarnate consciousness, now finding itself discarnate, learns to transform and expand itself into the spaciousness and powers of its inherent hyperdimensional nature. That metamorphosis from one configuration and organization of consciousness to another is what occurs in a part of the transitional realms called the Post-Mortem Realms. In effect these realms provide a continuation of the incarnation that just finished its physical phase. They are, in a manner of speaking, a spiritual half-way house between earth and the higher-order worlds.

In plain words, it's where the personality, freed from its body, learns to reunite with the soul that gave it birth. That reunion generally marks the departure from the Post-Mortem Realms and the true end of that incarnation.

The Post-Mortem Realms are expansive and diverse, offering a vast spectrum of possible environments and experiences through which an individual may integrate the lessons of his or her physical life and begin to acclimatize once again to life in the non-physical realms. Where a person goes upon death and what he or she experiences depends on a variety of factors, the most important of which is that person's overall state of consciousness and energy. The Post-Mortem Realms are themselves organized along an energy gradient that stretches from energy states close to those of the physical world to those that are equivalent to those found in the higher-order worlds. There is no reward and punishment system to this organization. A person goes to the level and environment most suited to his or her wellbeing, one that is resonant with his or her basic energy state and conducive to further growth, integration and wholeness. Because of principles of affinity, the new arrival in the non-physical realms will most likely be with people of similar mental and emotional states.

Basically, there are two major divisions in the Post-Mortem Realms. There are environments that are very earth-like, with landscapes much like you would find here in the physical world, with towns, cities, villages, rivers, oceans, mountains, and the like. These environments are created and maintained both by those who live within them and interact with them and by highly advanced angelic beings. Thoughts and feelings have direct creative impact in these realms; what was once invisible and subjective becomes the objective and very visible reality in the Post-Mortem Realms. Until an individual gains control over his creative faculties of thought and feeling, however, he or she may find himself or herself in an environment that is shaped and given consistency and coherency by larger planetary forces, similar to those Beings of nature that support our physical environments. In a sense they provide a scaffolding of familiarity and stability within which the newly arrived individual may begin to learn his or her way around.

John took me to meet one of these Beings once. It appeared to me as a woman, but I realized that what I was seeing was only a projection of a small part of its consciousness, configured to be accessible to me. It was a compassionate, caring Being, almost motherly, which I'm sure is why I saw it as female. It had created partly out of its own consciousness and partly out of the malleable substance of the

Post-Mortem Realms a landscape where a number of individuals lived who were healing from very traumatic and difficult livetimes on earth. I don't think any of those inhabiting this place knew of the existence of this Being, any more than most physical humans know of the many nature spirits and planetary Beings that energetically hold and support the environments we live in here on earth. But it knew all who were there within its loving care and did what it could to help them heal and move on to more advanced levels of the Post-Mortem Realms.

The earth-like half of the afterlife is itself divided into regions. The largest consists of environments familiar enough to a human mind that the individual can find his or her bearings in a comfortable and safe surrounding before venturing forward on the next stage of their development and reintegration with his or her soul. It looks like an earthly environment for the most part, but it is more spacious, radiant, and responsive to thought and feeling than we are used to here in the physical world. The individual knows he or she is in a non-physical world but one that is not so strange as to be disorienting.

Then there are numerous specific realms that I call the "belief worlds." Remember that an individual's mental and emotional state largely determines what he or she experiences, at least at first, in the Post-Mortem Worlds. Many people die with very firmly fixed beliefs about the nature of the afterlife or with other powerful beliefs about themselves and where they will be after death. It may be that the creative and formative power of these beliefs will bring that person into a place that mirrors them. A Christian may find himself in a place with churches or exclusively with other Christians. A Moslem may find himself in a place with mosques and other Moslems. In effect, birds of a feather really do flock together and will remain together as long as their consciousnesses need the familiarity and stability that such a "belief world" can provide. When they are done with that stage, they will move on, most likely into other area that are still earth-like but not as restrictive or constrained. They will find birds of other feathers.

There is no place of punishment as such, at least not a place where God or any higher-order Being punishes people for wickedness.

But we can be our worst judges and juries, and the punishments we can inflict on ourselves can be very severe through our thoughts and feelings of remorse, guilt, shame, and anger. Also, there are people who die enmeshed in very dark energies of hatred, fear, loathing, depression and selfishness. In the Post-Mortem realms these dark and destructive energies objectify and can shape the environment in which such a benighted individual finds himself. These places can seem like hell states, murky and dismal places where the individual is battered by the hateful forces he or she has been expressing in life towards others. This can certainly seem like punishment, but as soon as the individual realizes what he or she is doing and expresses even a tiny bit of remorse and a desire for Light, he or she begins the process of liberation from such "hell states," a process which will move as quickly as the person desires and is able.

In some cases, individuals may have woven such a strong pattern of constricted thoughts and feelings in life that they find themselves in a private realm constructed by their own habits. In watching the movies of Dicken's *A Christmas Carol*, I have often thought that if Scrooge had died, he would most likely have found himself in his counting house as usual though without Bob Cratchett, not knowing he was dead and going through the routine of counting his money over and over and over again, his consciousness held prisoner to the narrow routines he had developed in physical life.

In effect, we usually create the initial experiences of the afterlife we will experience while we are incarnated on earth. Merely being angry or depressed at the moment of death is not enough to take a person into one of these darker places. On the other hand, if anger and depression were habits shaping that person's inner life throughout his or her physical existence, then after death that mental and emotional shape, now objectified, will in turn fashion the environment that person will initially experience.

But such individuals are not left abandoned or without help. There are Beings who are specially trained to enter such realms without harm to themselves to minister to those in shadows and awaken them to their own capacities to generate a light that will move them out of the dark places. Even Scrooge would have been visited by someone, perhaps appearing as his nephew, his sister or even as his lost love, who would try to convince him of where he was and how he could be free—and that person would keep coming back for as long as it took, no matter how many times Scrooge would say "Humbug!"

Then there are those who are so attached to earthly life that they are unable or unwilling to detach themselves from it and become "earthbound," caught in the lowest levels of the transitional and realms where they overlap with the subtle environment of the physical plane itself. This earthbound state need not be due to negativity within the person. It arises due to the strength of the emotional or mental attachments the person has with something or someone in the phsycial realm, attachments he or she will not let go of to move on.

When my father died, I was concerned that he might become earthbound in such a manner. A very loving and kindly man, he had a strong conviction for many years that there were certain things he had to finish in his life before he died. At the time he died near the age of ninety, none of these things were completed, and I was concerned that the strength of his attachment might keep him hanging around in an earthbound state. This concern was heightened by the fact that I had had no knowledge of Dad's death when it occurred. We had had a lively and good talk just the night before. The next morning he had a heart attack.

Dad lived alone. Mom had died two years previously, and when she passed over, she immediately appeared to me in my living room two thousand miles away to let me know and to assure me that she was happy and well. Indeed, she looked truly radiant and joyous, having been freed from a body that was essentially bedridden at that point. But this didn't happen with Dad. There was no contact at all. Indeed, two days went by before a friend came calling and discovered his body, subsequently calling me to let me know what happened.

When my wife and I went back to Ohio to take care of the funeral arrangements, I entered his house with some trepidation, concerned at what I might find. But there was no trace of Dad's spirit or energy at all. Apparently he had moved on into the Post-Mortem Realms, and I was relieved.

About six months later, Dad appeared, sitting at our kitchen table, and had a short talk with me. At the moment of his death as he found himself standing in his bedroom outside his body, he saw a column of Light appear in the room. He said he knew he had to enter that Light immediately or he would succumb to the mental and emotional forces within him that would obsessively hold him in the house where his work and the things that he loved and needed were and thus close to the physical level. This is what he did, which is why he had not been able to contact me. For his own good, all links with the incarnate realm had been veiled until he could finally release his work obsessions and stand strong and free in his new life.

But there are others who are not so fortunate or aware as to seize the opportunity to move on and for a time at least they remain earthbound, not quite in the Post-Mortem Realms and not quite in the incarnate realms either. Yet even here, there are loving and compassionate Beings who seek out these individuals and help them move on. This is an area where many incarnate persons provide a service as well, offering "rescue" and liberation to souls who have been trapped by their own obsessive attachments. The television show *Ghost Whisperer* takes this kind of work as its theme.

The other half of the Post-Mortem Realms are those that are more oriented towards and similar to the conditions in the higher-order worlds. They are the "soul-like" realms. Here the individual's environment and personal form and function are more and more like those of the soul on its own level, leaving behind three- and four-dimensional modes of being and thinking and entering into the spaciousness—and qualitative difference—of the hyperdimensional realms.

At some point in this process, the individual may desire to enter into some form of service or help to the incarnate realms. He or she retains enough of a memory of physical life and incarnate consciousness and attunement to its conditions that links can be made with the mortal realm. Yet the individual is far enough into the realms of spirit that he or she can take on and mediate higher-order energies and perceptions. Such a person is like a new high school teacher who has just graduated from college. He or she is close enough in age and experience to the teenagers to understand their language and concerns yet possessing enough maturity to bring an adult's wisdom and insights to the classroom.

This area of service is not so much a realm as such as it is a function and a state of development. The individual is stable enough in a new life and environment to function well within it, yet at the same time wishes, before going further into the higher-order worlds, to go back and offer something to the world he or she has left. This is a purely voluntary choice. No one is ever forced to do this; it's not a requirement in order to move on. It's just that there's a level within the Post-Mortem Realms where such a choice is possible and opportune.

At some point, the individual is fully acclimatized, integrated, and able to blend gracefully back into the whole presence of his or her own soul and the work and life of the higher-order worlds. This is the "graduation" state. Again, it's not so much a particular level as it is a condition that the individual enters when participation in the Post-Mortem Realms is no longer necessary or required, except if the soul desires it as one who goes there to give service and training.

As I said at the beginning, this is a very simple overview. Given that the Post-Mortem Realms reflect and configure themselves to the consciousnesses of those within them, there is a potentially infinite variety of experience and conditions that one might encounter.

In terms of engaging with the subtle worlds, it has been my experience that the Post-Mortem worlds are where the strongest veils between the physical and non-physical worlds exist. Whole areas of these Realms are protected from influence and energies from the Incarnate Realms, and vice versa. The reason is not hard to understand. Individuals struggling to find their balance and stability in a whole new kind of life need to focus their attention upon what they are learning and doing and not be pulled back into contact with the world that they've left.

When she was sixteen, our oldest daughter spent a year on her own in Thailand as a Rotary Club foreign exchange student. The first few months that she was away, we were asked not to contact her at all short of an actual emergency. The reason was to mitigate the effects of initial homesickness. Experience had shown that when students kept in contact with their families from the start, they had a harder time overcoming homesickness and it took them longer to integrate into the culture of their host country. However, after three or four months had passed, we could have as much contact as we wished. A similar philosophy governs most contact with the Post-Mortem Realms.

And as might be imagined, there are veils and boundaries protecting physical individuals from the darker places within the Post-Mortem Realms and the energies of their benighted inhabitants.

Generally speaking, contact between the Post-Mortem Realms and our physical world is most common with those who are in a service mode. These are post-mortem individuals who may be actively seeking to communicate and work with physical persons and who are trained to do so. But again these are only general observations and principles, and there are always exceptions. Many people have regular contact with the Post-Mortem Realms while asleep, and others do so consciously through psychic and other means. And of course, the soul links we have with loved ones and friends continue and are conduits of connection no matter what realm or level the individuals are upon.

One interesting final Field Note before we move on. On almost all the occasions when I have had an opportunity to visit the Post-Mortem Realms, I have done so by seeming to cross a river. The mythic image of a river, such as the River Styx in Greek mythology, separating the realms of the living and the dead is powerfully ingrained in Western consciousness. Certainly there are energetic boundaries between the two realms, but whether the mythology of the river exists because those boundaries actually take the shape and function of a river or whether the river exists because so many human beings have imagined it over so many centuries is a good question and one for which I do not have an answer.

Field Notes Fourteen:
The Transitional Realms

Picture the higher-order worlds as a high-speed conveyer belt zipping along at fifty miles an hour carrying people from one place to another. To step onto this beltway from a stationary sidewalk is to risk stumbling and falling; the same risk is there stepping off. But if there are other conveyer belts between the high-speed conveyer belt and the sidewalk, and their speed goes up in increments of five miles per hour, then they provide a transition from standing still to going very fast and vice versa. The speed is stepped up or stepped down in smaller increments.

The transitional realms are like this intermediate beltway, mediating the energy differential between the higher-order worlds and the incarnate realms, allowing a smooth and graceful transition of energy and life between the two.

Another metaphor is that of our hands. When I write, for instance, the image of the story or book I'm working on and the ideas that form its content exist in my mind; they are real but they lack a physical form. Inspired, motivated and guided by these ideas and images, I sit at my computer, and my fingers play over the keyboard, creating symbols—words—on the screen. These words are the physical form of my ideas. Under normal circumstances, they are what you will read in order to encounter my ideas; unless we have some telepathic connection, you do not encounter my ideas as pure thoughts, feelings and concepts.

So in this metaphor my hands and fingers transform one form of existence—my thoughts—into another form of existence—my words.

That transformative function is the province of what I'm calling the transitional realms.

In point of fact, the actual transformation and mediation are not done by "realms" as such. These functions are performed by the consciousnesses and lives of the beings who live and work in these realms. Even calling them "realms" may be stretching it a bit. They may simply be aspects of the higher-order worlds that are accommodating themselves to the needs and characteristics of the incarnate, physical realms. The fact that in the subtle worlds "environment" and "state of consciousness" or "function of consciousness" are often synonyms of each other makes it challenging to make definitive statements. In this sense, what I experience as transitional realms and states may simply be the energetic byproduct or emanations of powerful planetary beings performing the transformative function.

This is the experience I had of the being who had created an environment within the Post-Mortem Realms (which are a kind of transitional realm in their own way). This environment, in which "dead" human individuals were living, was like a womb within this being, manifesting as a part of its total awareness and perhaps not a very large part at that. It was both a "place" and a "person," so to speak. It was an emanation of this being's compassion, love, and healing nature. It's as if a nurse or a doctor materialized a hospital for patients out of the etheric and energetic substance of his or her own body.

Earlier I used the metaphor of writing a novel to illustrate a point about incarnation. Let me return to that. The novel exists in my imagination—in my personal mental realm, so to speak—and there the characters are living their lives, having their adventures, working out the details of the story, and so on. This actually is how it feels to me, and I know it's the same for many other writers. The story and its characters come alive within me and in effect write the story, often taking it in directions I never anticipated and almost always better than I had imagined. In this way, I can experience the sense of having a semi-autonomous "world" living within me as part of my being yet not occupying the whole of me or my attention.

In many ways, the subtle worlds—or some of them at least—resemble for me the phenomena of cyberspace and the Internet.

Where exactly is cyberspace? What is it? It's very much like the Imaginal realm I wrote about in an earlier set of Field Notes. Most of my teaching is through the medium of the Internet. The organization I work with, The Lorian Association, maintains a set of virtual classrooms in cyberspace. These "rooms" have no reality at all in physical space; they are not located anywhere. People anywhere in the world who have access to a computer can take part in one of my classes, which is amazing and wonderful. And when we gather and work together in these classrooms, they become very real for all of us. I'm always amazed, in fact, at just how real, even though much of that reality is constructed in our own imaginations. Working in cyberspace has a lot in common with working in the subtle worlds.

When I teach a class online, the classroom in many ways becomes an extension of me and my own energy field, at least at first. In a very short time, it becomes a collective manifestation of the energy fields of all who are participating. This is a palpable experience, remarked upon by the majority of my students over the years. Something is created in non-physical space through our coming together and working together that takes on discernable and distinct energy characteristics, as fully real in its way as a physical classroom would be. There are obviously things we can't do in a virtual classroom that we could if we were physically together, but the reverse is also true. I have been consistently amazed, for instance, at how much more quickly an intimate, mutually supportive field emerges between us in cyberspace than if we were sitting face-to-face.

My point here is that what I call the "transitional realms" may in fact be nothing more than the field of energy—"the virtual" effect—generated by the activity of a variety of beings working together to facilitate the circulation of spiritual and vital energies between the higher-order worlds and the physical plane. Such fields move in and out of existence depending on the nature and intensity of the work that is being done; it's been my experience that there's a definite fluidity and plasticity—a malleability—about many of the places and conditions I've encountered in this transitional state.

On the other hand, sometimes these "virtual worlds" can seem very real indeed.

For instance, I've been to two areas in what I call the transitional realms that appear to be holding areas for vital energies both designated for and arising from particular species or parts of the world.

The most powerful of these appears to be a world entirely full of trees and nothing else. It's a realm of Forest, and from what I can tell, there are representatives there of every tree that exists or that has ever existed. Perhaps there are representatives of trees yet to make an appearance in the physical world as well, but I do not know that for sure.

I find this place to be overwhelming in its power and its beauty. It has an awesome presence, as if every tree in the world, no matter what kind, is part of a single, vast being whose manifestation is Forest. I have a special feeling for trees. They are among the most powerful and important species now on the earth, apparently one of the few who, like human beings, can reach directly into the higher-order worlds and beyond and invoke and channel subtle energies from those vaster levels of life. When I'm out for a walk, I always make a point of greeting and exchanging blessing with the trees that I pass. Sometimes when I do this I can feel the presence of this Forest in return. But it's when I stop and lean against a tree and just tune into it that I am most likely to find myself in this forest world, the soul-home for the tree against which I'm leaning.

Sometimes I attune to this place, to the presence of Forest, when I want to help a particular tree or group of trees. On one of my walks, for example, there are a few trees in a line that are on a spit of land that in effect is a narrow peninsula between a major highway and the road leading into my neighborhood. These trees are essentially cut off from other nearby trees and almost surrounded by roads. When I touch them, I can feel a certain sadness and loss of vitality because of that. I make it a practice to attune to them and then attune to Forest, calling down the blessing of that inner presence to these particular trees. The trees are not disconnected from Forest, but their environmental conditions make that connection weak. It's as if someone speaking to you in a soft voice is being drowned out by static and noise from the surrounding world. What I do is amplify that voice through my own attunement to it. I always receive a thank you and blessing in return from these trees when I'm able to do so.

The other "holding realm" that I have visited is one of stone and mineral, a world devoid of organic life but vibrant with the living energies within minerals. On the occasions when I have entered this place, it appears to me as a place of mountains and deserts, but I think that is because I love mountains so much and because I've lived part of my life in desert climates such as the American Southwest and have a love for the desert as well. In fact, at times this world looks to me like landscapes from New Mexico or Arizona but without the cactus or other plant life. It is a place of power and beauty in its own right, a place where the spiritual Light of the physical world is very strong.

On rare occasions in both these places, the world of Forest and the world of Stone, I have encountered nature beings who work there or at least tap into these archetypal places to withdraw vital energies that are then passed on to individual trees and to specific landscapes. But for the most part when I have been privileged to enter them, there is a spaciousness and purity unalloyed with any other consciousness or life except that of Forest and Stone. I suspect that these worlds are themselves contained and created by one or more vast beings who operate on a planetary scale. These realms seem to be intermediate states in the process by which the *idea* of forest and trees and the *idea* of stone and mineral are translated from the formative and creative consciousness of a being—perhaps the World Soul, perhaps something much more cosmic in nature, perhaps (and more likely) the Generative Mystery itself—into actual physical form and expression in the incarnate realm.

The transitional realms are the quintessential partnering realms. These realms—or the function from which they spring—are designed to facilitate energetic connection and partnering. They are designed to facilitate creative work with the differentials that exist in energy and consciousness between different and varied elements of the planetary system as a whole. If I wanted to use a bodily analogy, I would say that these realms are the circulatory system of the World Soul.

What kinds of beings inhabit the transitional realms? A nearly infinite number, really. There are beings whose entire function is one of transformation, making connections, enhancing circulation, and the like, and there are beings who perform that function when needed but who have other tasks as well and who may not spend much time in the transitional realms. As I understand it, every terrestrial species of plant and animal (including us) has its partner or partners within the transitional realms providing a connection where needed between that species and the organisms within it and the higher-order worlds. Because every organism, plant or animal, is part of nature, the most common designation for this wide panolopy of subtle workers is "nature spirits," though they may be known by other names as well in various cultures around the world. (In our own case, the primary link for each of us as individuals between our physical selves and our higher-order selves or souls is, as I've said, the "incarnate soul" or High Self. In a manner of speaking, this is our own private transitional being; more precisely, it is our soul performing a transitional function and acting as a transitional being within our individual incarnational system.)

Because of what they do, the work of these transitional beings (and thus the energy of the transitional realms themselves) extends into the subtle dimensions of the incarnate realms and brings them close to the earth. Although the energy of the transitional realms can reach nearly to the top of the planet's "energy hill," at this level where they meet and enter the planetary aura, their basic energy is only a step or two "upslope" of where we are most of the time. For this reason, transitional beings are among the easiest for us to become aware of or to contact as is evidenced by the rich folklore of interaction with these kinds of beings in all the cultures of the world.

Field Notes Fifteen:
Higher-Order Worlds

In the model that I've been using in these Field Notes, the higher-order worlds are on the "other side" of the Transitional Realms and constitute the complement to the Incarnate Realms. By now I'm sure you know that I call them "higher-order" not because they are necessarily superior or more highly evolved than the incarnate realms (though in some cases they certainly are) but because they exist in a higher number of dimensions than we do here in our four-dimensional world of spacetime. For this reason, as I've made plain, I also call them the "multi-dimensional worlds" or the "hyperdimensional worlds." These are the realms from which John came and many other beings with whom I work. And it is from these realms that many, if not most, of the subtle beings come who seek to aid the world and partner with humanity.

My model can be misleading in one important respect. The higher-order worlds and the incarnate realms don't really "orbit" each other like paired suns in a binary star system, nor are they arranged on a cosmic ladder with rungs in-between them. In effect, the higher-order worlds contain the lesser-order worlds within themselves. A five or six dimensional being contains within itself the three or four dimensions that make up our world. In effect, when the soul—a hyper- or multi-dimensional being—incarnates, it does so by creating or narrowing a part of itself to only function within three of the dimensions that are already part of its beingness. This constrained and contained part is what I call the "Incarnational Soul" or the "High Self," and it becomes, as I've said, the organizing matrix for the physical incarnation as well as performing the function of a connecting, transitional being within the personal incarnational system.

When John engaged with me, he did so by focusing his consciousness along and within three of the dimensions of his own larger being, which required energy and work on his part. When he took me journeying, he would in effect gather my three-dimensional consciousness comfortably within the spaciousness of his hyperdimensional energy field; I would become part of his own three-dimensional nature, riding within him like a kangaroo Joey riding in its mother's pouch.

The higher-order realms are essentially what we think of as the spiritual realms (although I would make a further distinction here, as I'll explain in a moment). These are the realms of soul and spirit, the home of those beings—gods, goddesses, teachers, masters, angels, devas, and so on—who serve, guide, guard, and nourish the development and evolution of life and consciousness on earth. These are the realms where we find our spiritual allies.

In an earlier set of Field Notes—the "Anatomy of a Contact"—I discussed the "flavor" or the "note" that emanates from a being due to its particular make-up and the way energy is configured within and around it. I use this flavor to distinguish between types of beings in the higher-order worlds; this energy pattern often determines (or is determined by) the primary function that a particular being is performing. Sometimes, it's a manifestation of where a being is from, which I'll explain in a moment.

As with the transitional realms, the higher-order realms are home to a near infinite variety of beings, many of whom—indeed, perhaps most of whom—have little to do with humanity; some I've encountered hardly know we exist (those encounters, though, have been very rare because since I'm a human being, I tend to attune to those beings who do work with humanity in one way or another). However, over the years, I've run into three main "flavors" of beings. There are undoubtedly more, but these are the ones with which I'm most familiar.

The first of these I think of as *Planetary* beings. By this I mean beings who work, mainly using the transitional realms, with the physical and energetic needs of the planet. These are the kinds of beings who generally are referred to as nature spirits, devas, and elementals. Their work is largely with nature and the evolution of form upon the earth.

These planetary beings deal with more than just nature, however. They also work in areas of sound, color, geometry, and pure vibration and energy in ways that we as incarnate humans have no experience of but which are vital to the processes of life and development within the planet as a living being.

These are the beings that generally attend to the circulation of energy throughout the whole planetary system. As such their work takes them regularly into the transitional realms, and many of them function and work out from environments they create in those realms, as I have already described. The Forest world may well be one of those environments used by those Planetary beings whose work is with trees. Many of them also work regularly with the subtle energies and environments of the incarnate realms. Those who do are in some ways among the easiest and most accessible of the subtle beings with whom one might engage, although their non-human nature and outlook can be a challenge to mutual communication and understanding. I shall have more to say about them in a later set of Field Notes.

The second "flavor" or general type of being I've encountered I think of as *Transplanetary*. The earth is part of a larger cosmic environment consisting of the solar system and the universe beyond. We see the physical expression of this environment in the sun and stars above us, but there is a subtle, non-physical counterpart as well. In effect, our world, Gaia, moves through the living fields of consciousness and energy of more vast and complex beings who are the souls of stars and galaxies, the most important to us being, of course, our own sun. As our planet does so, it absorbs subtle forces from these sources and offers its own energies back in a circulation of life and spirit on a solar and stellar level of consciousness.

The beings I call "transplanetary" are the ones who serve and enable this process. They act as intermediaries between the earth and its cosmic environment. They are the ones who take the more intense subtle energies and spiritual forces from solar and stellar sources and transform them into states that can be appreciated, assimilated and used by the beings who inhabit the various ecologies of our world, both physical and non-physical. Some of them appear to me to perform a function analogous to that of chloroplasts, the part of green plants that contains the chlorophyll that turns sunlight into food. Others seem to be messengers, carrying energies from our world to its celestial partners.

Once John took me to a region where this transplanetary work was in operation. To me it appeared as if we were in a high alpine meadow, a plateau of green grass high in the mountains with other mountain peaks around us. There was a cliff before us, and looking over, I could not see the bottom. Instead, all I could see were stars. It felt as if we were at the edge of the world, which in a sense we were for John said this was a boundary region between planetary and interplanetary and interstellar forces. Of course, what I saw and how I saw it were the way my mind interpreted the non-physical environment we were in.

As we stood there, I saw movement around us. Looking back, I saw that what appeared to me as grass were actually beings that rose up out of the "meadow," as if a green blade of grass in your lawn suddenly grew taller and larger than you. Once they reached a certain size, they seemed to launch themselves over the cliff or up into the air, heading out into the starry sky. One of these beings paused and stood with us, communicating briefly the idea that it was a messenger, carrying the life-energy and blessings of Gaia out into the interstellar community. It looked to me exactly like a giant blade of green grass, though with large eyes and the faint suggestion of a face around them. It had no arms or legs that I could see, but it had a shimmering corona of green light playing all around its form, from which tendrils of energy rose and swirled. There was nothing at all of human thinking or feeling about it that I could tell, yet I could sense strong purpose within it and an equally strong presence of love and joy. In a moment of whimsy, I dubbed this being in my own mind a "space elf." There was just something about it that felt "elvin" to me.

I have on occasion encountered beings coming from the other

direction, from solar or stellar sources. These are not extraterrestrials riding space ships but beings of energy. The ones from the sun always appear golden to me and are radiant with a loving, joyous energy. The ones from the stars vary in appearance but are most often for me a blue-white in color and electrical in feel, highly energetic and lacking in emotional resonance, very impersonal and non-human in their demeanor. There are, however, exceptions as some of the most loving beings I have ever encountered have been emissaries and teachers from stellar sources.

Transplanetary can take on another whole meaning as well, which actually has nothing to do with the higher-order realms but makes an interesting story nonetheless.

By way of prefacing this story, I should say that John once said that earthly humanity was a particular expression on this world of a sacred idea that was cosmic in its nature. As a consequence, there were other versions of "humanity" who might look nothing like us but who still fulfilled the same "niche" of consciousness within a planetary system that we did (or were attempting to do) on our world.

I was participating in a workshop with my friend R.J.Stewart, and he was leading us in an inner journey to a Hall of Records, a place like a library within the subtle realms. John had taken me to this place years before, so I was familiar with it. While R. J. was working with the workshop participants, I wandered off on my own down a corridor I had never seen before. At the end of it, I found myself in a large circular room that was open to the stars. At the center of it was a large well from which Light was emerging.

The feeling of this place was very similar to the Edge of the World location where I had met the grass-like "space elves." As I walked up to the well, I realized there were pathways extending out into the stars and that other beings were traveling along them. One of them, in fact, was very close and was also heading to the well.

This being was truly an alien, not one of the subtle beings who are part of this world. The energy around it was distinct and different from anything I had felt before, and I intuitively knew it came from another world. Like me, it was traveling in consciousness with its physical body back on its own home planet.

To my eyes, it looked like a giant snail, though its "shell" was more integrated into its body, most likely not a shell at all. It had features of a kind on the upper side of its body, the "snail" part, and it moved like a snail, gliding along on a great pseudopod. Along the side of its "face" was a fringe of what looked like small tentacles, and I had the impression that these could be extended when needed and used as I would use my hands and fingers. It had something like an apron draped in front of it which seemed to represent its "clothing."

Overall, this Being was beautiful and graceful. I felt a loving and welcoming vibration from it and also a sense of wonder; after all, it was meeting an alien, too, and probably unexpectedly. I got a distinct message of greeting and an explanation of why it was there. As I interpreted it, it was like a "junior" or "apprentice" priest, or something equivalent, on its world, and it was learning to project its consciousness out of its body to journey in much the same way I was doing. What I saw as a well was a representation of a particular source of universal Light and wisdom, and the task of this being was to commune with it and bring its energy back to its mentors.

What most struck me about this encounter was the feeling I had that I was in the presence of another human, a person like myself. It looked nothing like a human being but I felt a kinship with it as if we were both the same kind of creature. There was a resonance between us such as I feel with other human beings but different from what I feel with, say, an angel or a nature spirit. Had I had my eyes closed and simply felt the presence of this person, I would have said he (for it felt masculine) was a fellow human.

Thinking back on this later, I realized that this experience only confirmed for me what John had said years earlier, that humanity wasn't a particular form but a presence—an idea and a function— that could be manifested in a wide variety of forms adapted to very different evolutionary and environmental conditions on other planets.

Was I seeing an actual alien? I believe so, but it may have been a construct created by my imagination as a way of interpreting a form and pattern of Light and energy that otherwise would have made no sense to my earthly mind. I may well have gotten some of the details wrong; was it really a shell that I saw, for instance, or something analogous but actually quite different? I don't know. But the sense of this being's presence and intent was very clear and the fellowship we shared was strong, and in the end, that was what mattered.

The third "flavor" I've encountered has been the most common and numerous of my contacts. I think of them as *Spiritual* beings because their attention and function are focused on the development and quality of spirit and consciousness within the infinite forms that life can take. John for me was an example of such a Spiritual being.

As I've said already, *spiritual* is a word that carries a lot of different meanings and expectations. On the one hand, it is often used as a synonym for *non-physical*: if it's not part of the physical world, it's part of the spiritual one. But it's also used to denote holiness or sacredness, a higher level of being and consciousness. All subtle beings are non-physical by definition and all of them have an innate sacredness, just as we and every other physical being does as well. But not all higher-order beings have as their primary work the care and nourishment of the interior life of the world. What I mean by "Spiritual" beings are specifically those who nourish and support the spirit within us—and within all things. They are concerned with the development of life and consciousness independent of the forms through which they manifest. This "flavor" of beings includes the teachers and guides of humanity and of non-human life as well. For the most part, these are the angels.

In one way, all the higher-order realms are "spiritual" in that they embody spacious, loving, energetic levels of consciousness attuned to the Sacred. To designate one group as "spiritual" is not to mean the others are not. It is only to highlight that certain classes of beings actively focus on the spiritual and sacred life of the planet as their particular work and on the circulation of spiritual life and energy throughout the planetary system. These are usually the kind of beings we seek to contact and partner with as allies, and they are the ones most likely to be seeking to partner and ally with us as well.

These three designations of Planetary, Transplanetary and Spiritual are based on the way I sense energy patterns within and around beings. For that reason, this is a personal designation, part of my own internal mapping and based solely on my own experiences. Over the years, it has served me well, but you may have different experiences or choose to name things differently. I am certainly not intending to create any kind of rigid map or hierarchy here.

But I do feel it is important that we realize there are distinctions in the subtle realms and that these matter. They make a difference. Energies flow and are generated and things happen because of these differences. It's not enough simply to say, "Oh, that's an angel." What does "angel" mean to you in terms of an energy experience? What kind of angel is it? What distinguishes it from other angels or from other kinds of beings?

In the next set of Field Notes, I offer my thoughts about these differences in the form of my personal "subtle zoology."

Field Notes Sixteen:
A Subtle Zoology

As I have described earlier, I have been aware of non-physical beings since I was a very young child. One effect of this is that I never learned to see subtle beings through a religious lens. To me, they are life-forms. They exist in a different reality than I do, but they are comparable life-forms nonetheless. I came to see them in zoological rather than spiritual terms.

So from that point of view, what does a "subtle zoology" look like?

At first, I had thought to include this information in the previous sets of Field Notes by pointing out the kinds of beings that one might encounter in each of the realms I described. But I realized that in fact for most of the subtle beings I've encountered over the years, this was not possible. Like commuters, they might work in one realm but have their "home" elsewhere.

Remember that the various realms that make up the ecology of the subtle worlds are all states of consciousness, each of which creates or influences a corresponding environment. All beings have a particular "native" state of consciousness which defines their natural setting in the subtle worlds; for instance, our native incarnate consciousness makes us at home in the material universe and enables us to engage and interact with it.

But many beings can expand upon or alter their native state, which enables them to function in a variety of "places" in the subtle worlds. So to say that a being is found in the higher-order worlds or in the transitional realms or even in the subtle fields of the physical world may be misleading. It may actually occupy or have access to a much wider spectrum of states and "locations" than that.

For instance, a being with whom I have frequent contact appears to me almost always in the form of a brown bear. In a shamanic tradition it would be called an "animal ally" or a "power animal." Its bear form relates to particular qualities which it embodies.

Bear normally looks to me every bit like a large brown bear. Sometimes, though, he appears as a grizzly, standing very tall and looking very powerful, and once he appeared as a polar bear. He has never explained why he changes from time to time, but I get the impression it's just for fun, like we might dress in a different style now and again for the novelty of it. But once I asked him what he really was and what he really looked like. Was he really a bear?

In response, he suddenly changed, growing very large indeed, swelling up to maybe twenty or thirty feet in height with stars appearing around his head. "I can be a cosmic bear if I wish," he said, and then he changed altogether, dropping his bear shape and appearing as a very complex pattern of energy swirling around a radiant core of Light. He had stepped out of the form he used in the transitional realm and was showing me his form as a native of the higher-order worlds, specifically as what I've called a "Planetary" being.

This form is awesome and beautiful, but I have to admit, I find it easier to relate to him as a bear! But why is he a bear in the first place?

When nature spirits, for example, seeking to work with plants enter the lower transitional realms where they blend with the subtle realms of the physical world, they regularly take on energetic elements from the world around them. This is not an arbitrary action but a mechanism to allow *identification*, the blending of the nature spirit with the particular plant. This allows energy to flow more easily between them. The effect, though, is to make the nature spirit plant-like in its appearance. It's a reason that clairvoyants often see such spirits in a form that mimics or mirrors the physical appearance of the plant itself.

Thus the nature spirits that work with a large maple tree in my backyard can look like maple tree spirits because they take into themselves energetic elements—*"energenes"*—that are part of the subtle make up of the tree itself. If I see those nature spirits in their "true" form, they are bundles of Light, reflecting the complex, hyperdimensional geometry of their higher-order nature, but operating in the transitional realm, they become something more focused. Taking on the *energenes* of the tree enables them to do this.

This happens in the relationship between such beings and ourselves. Unless the being has a strong core identity that it can successfully project into our world, it may anchor itself in our presence and relate to us by taking on some of our *energenes*. This can have odd effects. If a person's field is largely made up of negative, hostile, angry energies, the subtle being can take on these characteristics, too, and manifest them back. We might say, "Oh, we're in the presence of a demonic being." But that same subtle being can then go into the presence of someone who is radiant with love, joy, and attunement to higher-order energies and take on *those* energies instead. Now we would say, "oh, a being of Light, maybe an angel, is with us!" Yet in both cases it is the same entity.

At some point, then, the being I call Bear may have been a nature spirit for bears, interacting with bears and their energy, taking on their "energenes" in the process and becoming shaped accordingly. At least in relationship to me, it is now functioning as a spirit helping a human being, but its bear form remains as its customary mode of contact with the physical subtle realms. This is speculation on my part, I must admit. When I've asked Bear, he just says he likes being a bear as it puts him in touch with interesting qualities. And then he growls! Bears can be touchy.

The fact is, though, that in thinking about a "zoology" of subtle life forms, we have to take into account that unlike physical creatures, subtle beings can and do change shape and may have multiple shapes depending on their various functions and connections. This doesn't mean that everything is chaotic and without any order and that nothing has any continuity of identity; there is a great deal of order. There are boundaries, and beings have cores of identity that are coherent and persistent. Yet their boundaries are often more permeable and interactive than we are used to on the physical plane, and the order and organization of the subtle worlds can be more dynamic and fluid than we experience here, except perhaps in dreams when we are exposed to the flowing, changing, transformative nature of a subtle reality.

Keeping this in mind, it is still possible to observe certain specific categories of beings, generally organized around function. So here's my list.

Angels

Angel is a term popularly used to refer to a wide variety of beings, from dead humans now residing in the afterlife to God's messengers, heralds and helpers in sustaining the universe. For me, an angel is part of a class of beings whose function is to foster, nurture and protect life and consciousness within the world. They are the gardeners of the interior life within all things. They assist us in remembering our oneness with the Sacred. They empower and nourish the evolution of spirit. Wherever consciousness is, there are angels. They are for me more God's shepherds than messengers, though they can serve that latter function as well.

There are many species of angels, including those who work exclusively with humanity. Among these are angels of nations, angels who overlight cities and towns, and angels who overlight organizations. For example, I have on occasion met angels that overlight corporations. Wherever human beings congregate and gather, joining their consciousnesses together in some common enterprise and thereby creating an opportunity for collective growth, angels will be present to foster that opportunity. They are in my experience radiant, loving, and powerful beings who guide, guard, and nurture the evolution of life and consciousness on earth.

In addition there are angels who assist activities, such as angels of healing, angels of protection, angels of sound and color, and angels who overlight artistic endeavors. The latter are the beings known in classical times as the "Muses."

Devas

Closely related to angels are the *devas*. Indeed, they may well be part of the same overall class of being but in this case focusing upon the non-human side of evolution and in particular upon the structural and formative energies and activities that help form the planet and which manifest as the laws of nature.

The devas and angels I have encountered are very similar in appearance; *deva*, after all, simply means "shining one" in Sanskrit, and this description could very easily apply to angels. They may be the same being, but with the "deva" being the non-human aspect and the "angel" being the side of their nature that engages with humanity. One being may fulfill a variety of functions.

However, on the whole, I feel a different energy signature or vibration from devas than I do from angels. The devas seem to me particularly aligned with the flow and circulation of life and vital energies, as well as being the architects and artisans of form. They are custodians and overseers of natural energies and forces, such as electricity. While I associate angels with cities, for instance, I associate devas with mountains and forests, rivers and streams, continents and oceans. They are the overlords of the wild places, whereas angels engage with civilization. That may, indeed, be their primary difference; that alone could account for the difference in feel and energy that I experience between them.

Nature Spirits

The comparison is often made that devas are the architects of nature while the nature spirits are the field workers and construction hands. It's an apt comparison, though perhaps a bit too human in its implications. The nature spirits are the transformers of life, taking the raw, intense subtle energies coming from the higher-order worlds and stepping them down into forms that can be appropriated and used by the subtle bodies of physical entities, mainly plants but animals as well. There are even "nature spirits" that attend to human beings, though we often call them "guardian angels."

Nature spirit is really an umbrella term, a bit like saying *animal* or *plant*. It simply denotes a being that works with the spiritual and energetic side of nature. However, just as there are billions of different species of plants and animals on earth, so there are at least that many different kinds of "nature spirits." In some ways, it's a meaningless phrase because it's so broad and all-encompassing.

In a manner of speaking, these kinds of nature spirits are analogous to bees, receiving the higher-order energies, digesting and assimilating them, and then producing from themselves an equivalent energy, like honey, which the plant can absorb within its vital subtle field. Of course, this is just a metaphor, not an exact description of what happens, but it conveys the principle of it.

A nature spirit is usually a being that is defined by a particular relationship with some specific form or function within the natural environment of the earth. By necessity, such beings, while their origin and fuller natures may be in the higher-order worlds, take form and work within the transitional realms and the subtle energy fields of the physical world. They tie themselves to specific landscapes and to geographical features such as rivers, and to species of plants and animals, and even to the individual plants themselves. The large maple trees in my backyard, for instance, have one or more nature spirits—in this case, maple tree spirits—associated with them.

Most nature spirits, then, are incarnated into the earth in ways that many of their subtle counterparts in the higher-order worlds are not. They have a more intimate relationship with matter and form. If I think in a metaphor of circulation and blood flow within a human body, they are part of the transfer mechanism that delivers nutrients from the blood stream to the individual cells and in turn bring the contributions of the cell back to the blood stream to become part of the larger whole of the body, as well as removing and eliminating waste products. Nature spirits are a vital, intimate, and "hands-on" part of the circulation of Light and vital energies through the planetary body of Gaia.

Human beings are part of nature, a fact we often overlook or forget, and as such, there are nature spirits "assigned" or related to us. Some of these work with our bodies, while others work with the products of our civilization. These are the spirits of our artifacts, the things we create and fashion from the materials we draw from nature. As human beings have advanced in this regard, becoming more and more technologically adept and transforming more and more of the natural world into forms and materials created by humanity, nature spirits have adapted to keep up. In this way there has evolved a whole new class of "nature spirits" that might be called "techno-spirits."

Techno-Spirits

These are the beings who inhabit or associate with the things that we make: the spirits of houses, for example, and of other buildings. Anything a human being crafts or manufactures creates an energetic niche, to use an ecological term: an environment that may potentially generate—usually through association with human beings and their energies—enough stimulation and energy to be attractive to some type of subtle being. I called these "tidal pools" in an earlier set of Field Notes. The development of human civilization has brought into being a whole new mode of evolution for nature spirits, creating hybrid beings who are not quite part of nature and not quite part of humanity but occupying a middle ground between the two. Whereas human beings once lived in forest, jungles, and savannahs, now well over half of humanity lives in urban environments. Before we reach the middle of the Twenty-First Century, it's estimated that over eighty percent of humanity will be clustered in cities. In these increasingly complex and energy-rich environments, whole new types of "urban spirits" have evolved and developed. Technically, they are still "nature spirits," I suppose, but in appearance and energy, they have evolved into practically a new species, one that performs many of the same functions as their country cousins but in new ways and with some new functions added. An analogy might be whales who are biologically mammals the same as human beings or dogs or horses, but who have evolved very differently by virtue of living in the different environment of the ocean.

As we increasingly confront the environmental challenges of the next few years and decades, humanity would benefit by seeking collaboration with the higher-order worlds, but in particular we may need the help of the nature spirits and their urban cousins, for it is their environments that we are increasingly destroying or altering. They hold the powers of healing and transformation that we may greatly need in the future. Research and study in the ways of cooperation and partnership with these beings, both within nature and within our cities and associated with our technologies, will be important, perhaps along the lines pioneered by the Findhorn Foundation community in northern Scotland.

Elementals

The boundary between elementals and nature spirits is a vague one. Sometimes elementals are called nature spirits and vice versa. They may, in fact, be part of the same class of beings. But they feel different to me, so in my own mapping of the subtle worlds and their denizens, I distinguish between them. It may simply be that elementals are a more specialized form of nature spirit.

Elementals are among the most powerful of the subtle beings I've encountered but also in some ways the simplest or least complex. Their power comes in part from the singleness and purity of their nature, as they manifest a single function or purpose unalloyed with anything else. They work with fundamental forces of nature and creation. If devas are the architects and nature spirits (or urban spirits) the contractors, then the elementals are those who lay and maintain the foundations.

It is this purity of purpose and function and their association with truly basic, foundational forces that gave them their name in European medieval writings describing the beings of the subtle worlds. The world was thought to be made up of four basic elements: earth, air, fire, and water. Therefore the beings associated with each of these elements became known as the *elementals* or spirits of the elements.

There are devas of the elements as well, and it's possible that the elementals themselves are fractal offshoots of these higher-order beings. In effect, these beings represent active principles at work in the world: contraction, concentration, stability, and solidity for earth; flow, adaptability, and merging (though dissolution) for water; purifying, energizing, and transformation for fire; and spaciousness, release, expansion, and holding for air. In European magical traditions, these elementals are called the salamanders for fire, undines for water, gnomes for earth, and sylphs for air.

The way in which a particular being, whether elemental or nature spirit, is seen and experienced by a human can depend on the environment in which that person lives and his or her cultural imagination since these beings often "clothe" themselves in forms and images taken from our imaginations and our energy fields in order to contact us. Sometimes this can take unexpected forms.

I lived for a number of years in Arizona, where I loved going out into the desert. I moved away when I was twenty and went to California to begin my work as a spiritual teacher, but I always had a sense of connection to the vitality and spaciousness of the desert. Many years later when my family and I moved to the Puget Sound area in the Pacific Northwest, I did what I always do when I go into an area and attempted to introduce myself to the local nature spirits and devas. To do this, I sat in my office one day and began tuning in to the environment around me, to the mountains that surround the Sound, to the forests, the water of Puget Sound itself, and so on. But I was having little luck. Try as I might, I could not connect.

As I sat there in my chair, I was aware that a being had just come into the room and was standing behind me to my right. Turning, I saw to my surprise that my visitor was a tall being, about seven feet or so in height, and broad, looking very much like a kachina, one of the powerful nature spirits from the American Southwest. Why this being appeared I had no idea, but it became my intermediary for a time with the local nature beings of Puget Sound. When I asked why it had come, all it showed me was an energy link between the mountains of the Northwest and the deserts of the Southwest. It wasn't until years later that I realized that my kachina was in fact a fire elemental, which given the amount of fire energy in the Puget Sound area due to the many volcanoes around us was entirely appropriate. And I realized that I had apparently unconsciously formed an association with this fire being during the many years I spent camping and walking in the Arizona deserts.

Based on my own observation, I suspect elementals may be emanations of the planet itself, embodying the energetic power of the physical world rather than, like the nature spirits, bringing and transforming subtle energies from higher-order worlds and the cosmos beyond. I have no doubt that the elementals have universal connections and are part of the cosmic order of things, but nevertheless, they seem to me at times like true natives of the earth itself, emanations and manifestations of the incarnate world as much as of the higher, spiritual planes. Of course, this is at this time only speculation on my part, and much more observation and research is needed to confirm or deny this.

What prompts me to even consider this is that when I attune to or contact nature spirits, I am aware of their beings extending into or having links with the higher-order worlds. But when I commune with the elementals, I find my attention and energy being directed earthward, not in a bad or confining way but in a manner that suggests this is where they are drawing their power from, directly from the physical and incarnate life of Gaia itself.

Non-Physical Humans

As a human being, by far and away the majority of contacts I have in the subtle worlds are with other human beings who are living in non-physical bodies. This makes perfect sense. Other humans, particularly those who have had incarnations in the physical realm, are the ones who are most concerned with human development and wellbeing. Further, they have the most experience and wisdom to offer in ways that are relevant and appropriate to us.

As I mentioned in earlier Field Notes, some of these non-physical humans come from those parts of the Post-Mortem Realms that are engaged in service to the physical plane. They have the reason and training to do so and come to assist as partners and collaborators. It's possible, of course, to come into contact with "dead" individuals who have not progressed that far and who, in fact, may be earthbound, but this is not desirable or even the norm unless you are doing "rescue" work for those dead who are still trapped in the subtle energy field of the earth.

The most powerful and important non-physical humans are those who come directly from the higher-order worlds, as John did, perhaps taking on temporary forms or appearances in the transitional or imaginal realms in order to contact us. These include the many teachers, guides, adepts, Masters of Wisdom and Compassion, and so forth that are deeply engaged in helping in the overall evolution of humanity. And of course, there can be ties and links forged in loving and familial relationships in this and previous lives that provide pathways of communion and communication between souls on both sides of the incarnational divide.

The categories I've mentioned are the main types of beings with whom I've come in contact, but they don't exhaust the possibilities by any means. Earth's "second ecology" is rich with non-physical lives who don't fit into the classification of angel, Deva, nature spirit, elemental, or human. For example, there's a type of being that I've been aware of for many years but which I've only recently begun to study. They seem to me to be a subtle world equivalent of microbes or bacteria—very simple forms of consciousness and life that serve a function in "fixing" or anchoring subtle energies within the physical world. In a whimsical moment, I called them my "underbuddies," and the name has stuck for me. There is little I can say about them at this point as I don't know enough to be certain of what they are or just what they do, though I suspect their function is an important one. Perhaps in a future set of Field Notes, I'll be able to share more.

As it is, these Field Notes present only the briefest of overviews. My intent is to give you a sense of the subtle worlds as a true ecology, filled with life-forms manifesting in an almost infinite variety and forming a vast interconnected network of energy and consciousness. I have also wanted to keep my descriptions simple to allow plenty of room for you to make your own discoveries and insights.

I believe over the next few years it's going to be important to come to a deeper understanding and partnership with these subtle worlds and the beings within them, for they are part of the overall wholeness of the world and have great wisdom about how the world works. Given the complex global challenges that we face, our task in this century is certainly to learn how to manifest that wholeness in all that we are and do. Subtle beings can be our allies in this. It's what they want as well, to join with us in collaboration and partnership in service of Gaia and the sacredness within all things.

Other Evolutions

There are subtle beings that don't fall into any of the categories I've given above; I think of them as parallel evolutions. These are the beings popularly known as faeries and elves or in the Celtic traditions, as the *Sidhe* (pronounced shee). My friend R. J. Stewart, a Celtic scholar and an expert on these kinds of beings, calls them our "cousins" and has had extensive experience of encountering them, which he has written about in his books on the Faerie Tradition. Likewise, another friend, John Matthews, has also written an excellent book, *The Sidhe*, about these beings based on his own inner contacts.

These beings are often confused with nature spirits, and the term "fairy" is also commonly used to describe a particular kind of nature being. But a faerie is a different kind of intelligence and being altogether, a member of a race that is using the earth and its subtle realms for their evolution just as we are. In effect, they have their own unique world within subtle dimensions of the earth. There is a tradition that humanity and the faerie race share a common ancestry, but a split occurred and we moved more deeply into physical matter and they did not. Much like the whales who were at one time land animals and then returned to the oceans and evolved into sea-dwelling creatures, so the Sidhe and similar beings may have returned to the ocean of the inner worlds. Yet even so, they remain in contact with our side of the earth, expressing their love and attunement to nature and their deep affinity for and link with the true nature spirits.

Though I have had less contact with them myself than with other kinds of subtle beings, I do know that when approached with respect and love, they also are open to partnership with physical humanity for the benefit of the world.

Field Notes Seventeen:
Here Be Dragons

One of the most frequent questions I'm asked about engaging with the subtle worlds is this: "Is it safe?"

According to Hollywood movies and horror novels, it would seem the subtle worlds are filled with angry, hostile, evil, predatory entities just waiting to possess or harm us. In this view, to contact or engage with the non-physical dimensions is to place our wellbeing and even our immortal souls in jeopardy. In my experience, this danger is wildly overblown and overdramatized. The subtle worlds are no more filled with evil than an average city is populated only by criminals, muggers and evildoers. Most of the world is filled with interesting people who are friendly, kind and hospitable. The subtle worlds are no exception to this and if anything are even more open and benign. Engaging with the subtle worlds is generally no more risky than a walk in a forest or visiting a national park.

But as any policeman will tell you, there *are* criminals and evildoers in the world, and most cities have troubled and dangerous areas where caution needs to be exercised, assuming one goes into them at all. One can get lost in a forest if one strays off the trail without a compass or any woodland skills to help find one's way, and there *are* places in the wilderness that can be dangerous to a person who is careless or unprotected. For that matter, any environment, no matter how friendly it may be ordinarily, may become dangerous if we treat it or those who live within it ignorantly and without respect or concern for their welfare.

As I said in the beginning of these Field Notes, one of my objectives is to take away some of the glamour, the mystification, and the fear that surrounds the subtle worlds. These realms are the other half of earth's ecology, a "second ecology," and most importantly, our partners in planetary evolution. These days, with the complex and multifaceted global challenges facing human civilization, they are also our partners in salvation, in healing and bringing balance and health to the world system. They are our partners in ending the civil war that rages between the human part of nature and everything else. They are our partners and allies in restoring and sustaining wholeness.

But no partnership is possible where there is fear.

By the same token, no partnership is possible where there is only partial knowledge and salient facts remain hidden. Consequently, these Field Notes would not be complete without acknowledging that there are dangerous places and dangerous beings within the subtle worlds. On the map of the inner, there *are* conditions where it could be written: "Here be dragons…"

But before we look at what these "dragons" may be and where these places are, let me begin with a personal story.

When I felt the calling to leave college in 1965 and devote my life to spiritual work, I was assisted in implementing this by good friends who ran a metaphysical center in Los Angeles. They invited me to come to their place and give some talks and see what might happen. I did, John appeared, and the rest of my life is what happened.

My friends were professional psychics and channels, well-versed in working with the subtle worlds. As counselors, their primary work lay in helping people deal with troubling issues in their lives and in particular with negative energies. They often performed exorcisms to free individuals from negative entities and thought-forms that had attached themselves and were living parasitically on that person's subtle energies.

This was all new to me. I was like the innocent country bumpkin that comes to live with an urban policeman. Although I had certainly run into negative energies before around certain people or places, I had never encountered a negative or toxic subtle being. They simply were not part of my world. All my contacts with the inner worlds had been with positive, Light-filled and loving beings.

As I say, they had invited me to give talks dealing with my

experiences with the subtle worlds. Because my experiences had nothing to do with dark or parasitic entities, funny situations developed in which I would be in one room lecturing about the positive, joy-filled, loving nature of the subtle worlds, while my friends would be in an adjoining room performing an exorcism or giving a class on how to protect oneself from predatory inner beings!

Needless to say, this led to some interesting and lively discussions between us. My friends honored my perceptions and experiences but felt they didn't go far enough. They felt I was naïve in not taking the dark side of the subtle worlds seriously enough. I, on the other hand, feeling perfectly safe dealing with inner beings, felt they took the negative side too seriously and spent too much time doing rituals to protect themselves and their center. Indulging in a bit of metaphorical hyperbole, I saw the inner worlds as mountains kissed with sunlight and sparkling in the Light and they saw them as swamps filled with lurking things that bit and scratched and could pull you into the murk if you weren't careful.

Because we loved each other and had become good working colleagues, we ended up learning from each other and moving in each other's direction. Their "swamp" became less murky and my "mountains" developed some sharp, craggy, slippery places. In fact, participating in some of their work and exorcisms gave me important insights into the ways in which the subtle realms could be dangerous and definitely broadened my perspective.

As I said, they were like cops whose work by necessity brings them in touch with the darker and toxic side of the world and gives them experiences that normally a person would not have. That was not and is not my work, but I learned from their experiences.

I tell this story for two reasons. The first is to emphasize how different the experience of the subtle worlds and of subtle beings can be depending on what you bring to the process and the nature of your involvement and work. The second is to make clear my orientation. If you are looking for lurid tales of demonic beings possessing little girls (or anyone else for that matter), you won't find them here. If you want a detailed description of all the dark and shadowy realms or how to perform exorcisms to get rid of evil bad guys, you won't find that here either. None of that is part of my experience.

My friends in Los Angeles did not change my opinion of the subtle worlds as essentially safe and good places (nor did they want to or try to), nor did their perspective and experiences lead me to fear these realms. But I did learn to respect the potential dangers and to act accordingly. And I'm not entirely ignorant of the darker side; John made sure I understood what I was doing in engaging the subtle realms.

From what I've observed, what most people fear are attacks from evil and negative beings out to prey on humans. But I've found that most of the danger that the subtle worlds may pose does not come from evil or malevolence. It comes from carelessness and ignorance which can lead a person into engagement with subtle energies or states of consciousness that are more powerful or too different for him or her to handle. This is no different from going into a physical wilderness unprepared. Here in the Puget Sound area where I live, for instance, hardly a winter goes by that someone isn't injured or killed on the slopes of the Cascade Mountain range, often because they went hiking not fully prepared and got caught in a sudden and unexpected snow storm, a "white out" that left them freezing, confused, lost, and ultimately dead.

When as a teenager living in Phoenix, Arizona, I would go hiking and climbing in the deserts and mountains, I was aware that there were rattlesnakes and large poisonous lizards called Gila Monsters in the environment that could injure or kill me. In addition, there were treacherous areas in the mountains where rocks could give way under my feet leading to a fall. And in the summer, there was the heat which could kill me through dehydration or heatstroke. But simple precautions such as the right clothing and boots, taking plenty of water, and being careful where I put my hands and feet while climbing minimized all these dangers. I knew where rattlers were most likely to be and I avoided those areas when I could, all the time paying attention to my surroundings.

Most importantly, I was never afraid. I loved being in that environment. I loved the heat and I loved the ruggedness of it all and the fact that you could see practically forever in the clear desert air. Some of the most ecstatic moments in my life came while hiking in the desert or climbing among the crags and cliffs of the Arizona mountains. As long as I kept my wits about me, I was perfectly safe.

The subtle worlds are like that. They are simply an environment with their own nature and with lifeforms who make that environment their home. They have special characteristics due to their non-physical nature, to be sure, but nothing we can't be at home and safe with if we take a modicum of care and enter those realms with love and respect. After all, they really are our home—or one of them, at least, for as human beings, we are denizens of both worlds, metaphysical and spiritual amphibians living simultaneously in the physical world of our body and the non-physical worlds of our minds, emotions, and spirits. We should not approach one of our homes with fear.

I have two final thoughts before discussing just who or what the "dragons" may be and how to prepare for them.

This is a very large theme; I know of entire books written just about this one topic alone and about psychic defense and protection. In these Field Notes, all I wish to do is skim the surface. The idea and the images of dark and evil beings are already so vivid and fear-producing in people's minds thanks in large part to horror movies and television shows that I have no desire to add to these images or give them power. But as I said earlier, it's also a topic that cannot be wholly ignored.

Furthermore, as I suggested in the story I told above, it's not as if I have wide experience in dealing with dark forces. In sixty years of engaging with the subtle worlds, I simply have not encountered that many negative beings. I can't write about what I don't know.

With that preamble, let's start with the most dangerous place and the most dangerous beings I know. That place is our own personal subtle field and the beings are us, you and me. If there is any place where the phrase "Here be Dragons" should go, it should be stamped on our foreheads! By far and away we are more threatened by the negative energies we generate ourselves than by any negative beings of which I am aware.

There are three reasons for this. First, if a compassionate love and goodwill for others can find no room in our hearts and we are consistently hating, angry, vengeful, depressing, and negative in our responses to others and to ourselves, we generate and build up around us in our personal subtle field a miasma of toxic energy. It's like walking around all the time inside our own personal smog cloud. We may become so used to it that we cease to notice it, though others certainly will, but it will still impact us and our bodies.

Secondly, the energies of such a toxic personal field can break loose and become thought-forms existing in the Imaginal realm. Most likely they will remain hovering about their creator, feeding on his or her negative energy and reinforcing it. In a sense, the individual becomes possessed by a subtle creation of his or her own making. When I was working with my friends in Los Angeles, the majority of exorcisms and "clearings" that they did for people were of this kind, getting rid of negative thought forms that the individual had created at some point and which now were afflicting him or her.

If there's enough energy of will, thought, imagination, and emotion behind them, they can gain a kind of loose autonomy, become a "floating" negative energy field that can attack or attempt to infect others. Such thought-forms cannot stay in existence unless "fed" and energized in some manner. One way for them to do this is to attach to the energy field of someone whose thinking and feeling has a resonance with them and thus provide them a mental and emotional home. Another way is to find their way out of the Imaginal and into a band of feral energies within the planetary subtle realms that I call "The Scream." I'll discuss that more in a moment.

Thirdly, we often see the world energetically through our own auras. If they're murky, then the world will appear murky to us. People who see the world as a fearful, evil place may be projecting onto the environment (and onto others) conditions and qualities that actually are present in their own minds and hearts and in their personal subtle field. This is bad enough. But if the individual sends his or her consciousness into the subtle realms, then his or her inner state becomes mirrored and reproduced in this new environment. In the subtle realms of the earth and the lower transitional realms our thoughts and feelings go a long way to shaping the actual environment a person experiences. This is particularly true in the Post-Mortem Realms after death, a phenomenon that gives rise, as I wrote in an earlier set of Field Notes, to the darker, shadowy places within those Realms that reflect the negative emotional and mental conditions of those who are in them.

But a person need not die to experience this phenomenon at work. If I have toxic, angry, hateful, negative thought-forms in my aura, then when I attune to the subtle worlds and project my consciousness into them, suddenly those thought-forms cease to be subjective and "inside" me but are now objectified and outside of me. My experience may then be one of encountering—and possibly being attacked by—negative or evil "beings." The truth is that I am attacking myself through the instrumentality of my own self-created thoughts-forms, but it takes a depth of self-knowledge and honesty to clearly see this when it is happening, much less do something about it.

And what can be done about this situation?

A prerequisite is willingness to change, the honesty and self-knowledge to know what needs changing in one's self, and then putting forth the effort and energy to make the change. Given that, remember that all thought-forms are creatures of energy. Deny them energy, and they die. This means changing habits of thought and feeling that would otherwise feed them. It means substituting forgiveness for anger, love for hate, acceptance for rejection, self-respect for self-loathing. In effect, you change the "psychic Ph" of your personal subtle field, just as chemically and biologically you can often get rid of bacterial and viral infections by changing the acid balance of your bloodstream and body. Make an environment chemically, biologically, and energetically inhospitable, and an organism—whether physical or non-physical—that might otherwise thrive in it will be repelled or die.

In this regard, treating toxic energies and thought-forms in one's own aura is greatly helped not only by changing to positive, constructive thinking and feeling but by simple physical exercise (particularly if it is sufficient to stimulate the production of endorphins by the brain) and taking constructive actions to help others.

Depending on the nature and severity of the psychological habits that are creating the negativity for the individual, he or she may do well seeking professional therapy to heal and change these habits. Of course, asking for help from one's own soul, from the Sacred, and from spiritual allies doesn't hurt either! I also ask for angelic assistance, for there are angels particularly tasked with helping human beings clear away this kind of toxic material.

The irony is that for all the stories about evil beings lurking in the unseen worlds, the places people are most likely to encounter unpleasant, negative or even dangerous subtle energies are of our own creation right here on earth among other physical human beings. Like television broadcast stations, we fill the environment around us with unseen energies generated by our own thoughts, feelings, and spiritual activities. For the most part these are neither strong nor persistent enough to cause any problems; there is not a great deal of intention or focus behind them. Further, if the subtle energies in our environment are clear and circulating naturally like breezes through a room, they draw our energies into their flow, sweeping them into more spacious domains.

When our thoughts and emotions are more intense and focused, especially if there is clear intentionality behind them, then the subtle energies we generate can last and become part of the subtle environment itself. In a positive way this can bless an environment and give it a persistent good "atmosphere" or feel to it. However, if the energies we're putting out are consistently negative and hurtful, then a toxic situation can develop within the subtle fields of that environment. It's like pollution of any kind. It renders an environment unpleasant at best and dangerous at worst.

I remember once visiting a store where a friend of mine worked. He was having a very bad day, and when I walked in, he was seething with anger. I could see spikes of red energy shooting out from his aura like spines on a porcupine, and his co-workers were staying away from him. It was obvious they were feeling the impact of his angry energy on their subtle bodies, as well as picking up on his grumpy mood. I asked if he could take a break (he was a manager of the store), and I whisked him next door to a coffee shop for a cup of tea and a chat to calm him down. As we talked through some of what was bothering him, the "spines" disappeared and his energy field calmed down. He returned to work no longer an "energy porcupine," much to the delight of his co-workers.

This was a one-time situation, but had he made a habit of bringing such an angry energy to work, it could well have built up within the subtle atmosphere of the store, making it uncomfortable both to work and to shop there. If the employees then became angry and grumpy in response, it would only add to the problem.

Some environments have better circulation of subtle energies moving through them than others. Natural settings are the most beneficial in this regard, whereas many buildings and rooms because of the way they are built can become "energy traps," places where subtle energies stagnate unless an effort is made to keep an energetic flow going. Negative thoughts or feelings in such energy-constricted places can build up a toxic psychic atmosphere. A prison could be one example of this, though I have found these conditions existing in otherwise well-lit office buildings that were still constructed in a manner that impeded the flow of subtle energies.

Hospitals, for instance, are places where people regularly experience fear, anger, despair, depression, and pain, as well as the more positive emotions of giving service and providing healing. I have been in hospitals where the subtle atmosphere has not been attended to and negative energies have built up over time. I can hardly wait to get out. When I needed to have a series of surgeries a few years ago, I picked a hospital that was inconveniently distant from where I live but which had a splendid subtle energy field. For whatever reason, this building and the subtle environment within and around it felt fresh whenever I visited it, which greatly augmented the healing power of the place, at least as far as I was concerned. I was more than happy to travel the extra distance to be treated in such an energetically vital and clean place.

Here's another example. When I was on the lecture circuit many years ago, there was one center I visited regularly which was very popular. It was housed in an old building with multiple rooms which were used for different workshops and classes. Few of the rooms had any windows to the outside. Many of the workshops were psychological in nature and involved people "letting go of their feelings" and emoting and doing cathartic exercises. This was releasing for them, but the energies they dumped stayed in the rooms until psychically they became stale, sluggish, and "sooty". No one ever did any basic energy hygiene to cleanse the rooms after they were used in such cathartic ways.

At first I didn't realize what was happening, only that doing workshops in this center and trying to move the energies of the people I was working with was more difficult than it needed to be or should have been. One of my allies let me know what was happening, and I did a cleansing, which helped enormously. I later told the management of the center about this situation. They promised to take necessary steps for energy hygiene, and things did get better after that.

Energy awareness and energy hygiene are not skills we are regularly taught in our culture, so we do not make a conscious effort to clean up our subtle energy environments; yet, one person skilled in this way and consciously invoking a circulation of spiritual energies can make a real difference in many of these situations. Just a simple act of blessing a room when you enter it can be important.

But sometimes, the toxic subtle energies have accumulated for so long and have so imprinted themselves upon the physical environment that stronger measures are necessary to clear them out. That is a topic beyond the scope of this book.

As I said earlier, we each have natural subtle immune systems or energetic boundaries that act in protective ways. Both of these factors greatly mitigate any negative effects that might be present in most average energy environments. We should not go through our days fearful of running into negative energies. We actually would have more to fear from our own fear in such a case and its deleterious effect upon both our physical and subtle bodies than from any subtle forces we might encounter.

There are inner beings whose primary function is to "sweep" areas clear of such stuff and keep Light flowing and circulating, otherwise we would long ago have drowned in our own negative psychic effluvia and energy sewage. And we can do our own sweeping as well. Love, joy, happiness, compassion, honor—again all the usual positive suspects—are powerfully transmuting and cleansing forces radiating from us. Animals and plants can also exert healing and transmuting energies. Music can be a powerful cleansing force as well.

When I did a weekend workshop in Britain with a friend of mine, William Bloom, it was held in a very old building. The subtle energies there weren't outrageously negative but they were stale and depressing. William, who is very skilled at working with subtle forces, began the weekend by putting everyone to work physically and energetically cleaning the rooms we would be using. Not only did he play music while we worked, but he had everyone sweeping, washing the windows, mopping the floors, scrubbing the walls, all with an attitude of bringing Light and vitality into the old place. It transformed the feel of the surroundings and brought a lightness to the workshop that might not have been there otherwise had we had to contend with the dreary feeling the building had had when we first arrived.

Earlier I mentioned a "feral band of energies." We are all aware—unfortunately—of pollution. I remember back in the Sixties flying into Los Angeles and feeling my lungs cringe as I looked out the window at the orange cloud of pollutants and smog that we were descending into. Nor does this kind of pollution necessarily stay in one place, for there are no boundaries in the air. A friend of mine who was a pilot in Arizona said when he was in the air, he could see streams of smog flowing eastward from Los Angeles and settling into the Salt River Valley that was the home of the city of Phoenix.

Again unfortunately, there's a kind of psychic or energetic pollution that flows around the world as well within the subtle fields of the incarnate realms. It is a band of "feral" energies born of the suffering, the pain, the fears, and the negativity of humanity. I call it "the Scream" as it feels like a scream from the collective consciousness of humanity.

Let me be very clear here right away. There is no reason why you would enter this band of negativity as part of your process of engaging with the subtle worlds or non-physical beings. Although it is a non-physical phenomenon, it is not part of the subtle worlds at all but an effluvium of energy arising from human suffering. It does not exist on the Imaginal realm, nor is it part of the transitional realms. It is part of the subtle energy surrounding humanity collectively and bleeding into the subtle fields of the earth.

It's the place where the thoughts and feelings generated by the deliberate wish to cause harm to another accumulate. There they are like free ions looking for something to attach to in order to "ground" their "charge." A person who has a strong, positive personal subtle energy field offers no place for such negative psychic ions to attach and thus is relatively immune to the worst effects of this band of energy.

This band is not like some cloud covering the earth equally everywhere. Because it is human-generated, it will tend to be more present where there are concentrations of people, but even then, its strength or influence can vary for it is subject to the effects of its environment. A city that is vibrant with health, creativity, parks, productive, happy people, good government, and the like is far less vulnerable than one where the population is depressed, angry, and fearful. The energies of this band are more concentrated in places where violence or abuse is taking place or where people are suffering, particularly over a prolonged period of time. Battlefields and warzones can be especially vulnerable to this feral energy, as one might expect.

This band of psychic energy is a problem that both incarnate humanity and those on the inner worlds seeking to help us have to deal with, for it is not always just a passive cloud of negativity. It can be a source of physical level aggression and hatred as individuals pick up on these violent energies and images and express them through action. It has the power to infect and transmit its toxicity to individuals who are vulnerable to it, which generally means individuals who, by virtue of their own hatreds and fears, are participating in and adding to this band of psychic energy themselves. It can also affect those whose natural psychic immunities have broken down in the face of prolonged suffering, depression or abuse. Under the influence of this feral energy, a person may have his or her own angers, fears and hatreds augmented and may take violent actions they would not otherwise engage in.

When horror writers envision evil unseen beings lying in wait to prey upon us, they are drawing for the most part on images born of the toxic nature of this band of psychic forces. In my understanding, aside from the effect of the polluted psychic energy itself, the most prevalent denizens of this band are malevolent thought-forms sprung from the hurtful imaginings of human beings and given a certain energetic persistence through an intensity of desire to see those images fulfilled. When a Shi'a Moslem sees a Sunni Moslem or an Irish Catholic sees a Protestant as an enemy, for example, and wishes that person harm, that kind of imagination and the emotion behind it is what creates the kind of toxic thought-forms that can populate this "Scream."

Early in my training, John took me, under his protection, into this band of energy so that I could experience it and know that it was there and what it was like. He said clearly that no one should be afraid of this region, particularly as fear is one of the emotions that can create a resonance with it, but it is something that exerts an influence upon humanity and thus can potentially affect all of us.

"It is part of the collective karma of humanity," he said, "a weight upon your consciousnesses until you can transmute it through love and goodwill towards each other." He then introduced me to beings whose main function was to bring healing into this region and prevent it from becoming too overwhelming a presence within the subtle fields of the incarnate world.

We are each born with a subtle, energetic immune system comparable to our physical one. Activities such as the four practices that John recommended help to maintain and boost it. The natural boundaries of our personal subtle field when strengthened by a healthy life style are usually more than enough to throw off any negative effects of the Scream. By deliberately drawing on your sovereignty and self-light and invoking the help of your soul and Pit Crew, you can avoid this unpleasant zone altogether when attuning to the inner realms.

But it is also part of the global challenge with which humanity struggles, as much as climate change, physical pollution, or any other problem. In some ways, it can be worse as it operates beyond the knowledge of most people and can diminish our capacity to deal with the problems that confront us, encouraging us to indulge in violence, fear or depression instead. One of the reasons for forming a partnership with the inner worlds is to join in the effort to mitigate, transmute, reduce and eventually eliminate this "Scream" from human experience. This is an important form of what I call subtle activism, which I'll discuss in a later set of Field Notes.

All of these sources of negativity and danger that I've discussed originate with humanity, not from sources on the inner. They are dangerous precisely because they already resonate with us; they come from imbalanced, wounded, hurting and hating parts of us. It's because these energies are of our creation that we are vulnerable to them and they can have power over us.

Are there, then, no negative or evil beings as such?

To say a being is "negative" can mean different things. It might be describing the actual energy and vibration of the being, but it may describe the impact of that being on us in a particular situation. A very loving security guard can seem gruff and threatening if we try to cross a boundary he's guarding.

So we need to define what we mean by "negative" here. What I mean by it is a quality of energy that breaks up and shatters wholeness and coherency, that is "hungry" and needy, and that seeks to diminish the life, energy and wellbeing of another. It makes the environment and those in it worse than they were before. It is often parasitic, using the life and vitality of others to sustain and further its own.

From the point of view of my contacts in the higher-order worlds, an evil being is essentially one suffering from a "pathology of identity." It has forgotten who and what it is as a spiritual being. It has forgotten its roots in the Sacred. In effect, its sense of identity has become free-floating and ungrounded, cut off from the Ground of All Being. Its identity feels unsupported and dependent on itself alone for survival.

This is a fearful condition, and at the core of most evil lays fear. Lacking connection to its Source in the Sacred, such a being must find other forms of support and does so essentially though hijacking and feeding on the identities of others. In a sense, evil is metaphysical identity-theft.

An evil or negative being is one who behaves like a virus, attempting to use a host to replicate and further its own energy. It has forgotten or lost its ability to align and sustain itself vertically with the Sacred and is now functioning entirely horizontally, so to speak, looking for sustenance, energy and power from others around it. And it gains that sustenance by attempting to exercise power and dominance over others, using fear and seduction to break down their boundaries of sovereignty and identity so it can infect them with its own identity, which is itself fearful at its core.

This pathology can take many forms and can lead to different strategies by means of which a being seeks to infect, dominate and feed on another's energies. Like a virus, it seeks to replicate itself within a host, for only through that self-replication can it feel its identity is secure.

The protection against such an entity, whatever form it might take or wherever it comes from, is to know one's own innate sacredness and connection to the Sacred. If I draw my sovereignty and sense of self from my soul and my connection to the Sacred, and if I am clear and strong in my boundaries and without fear, I can resist the infectious nature of such an entity. By mirroring back to it the presence and love of the Sacred, not fearing it but genuinely seeing it as part of God, I confront it with two choices. It can either remember its roots and be healed of its pathology, or it will fear those roots and retreat, for its pathological identity cannot survive once it remembers and accepts its own essential divinity.

This is why John said that before I engaged seriously with the subtle worlds, I needed to have a practice of attuning to self and attuning to sacredness. Self-Light rooted in and reflecting the love and presence of the Sacred is both the protection from and the response to negative entities.

Many years ago a young man came to me for advice. He had

been experimenting with contacting subtle beings and had in fact made contact with a source that seemed to be offering him good advice. It talked in terms of universal love and serving humanity and sounded like a highly evolved consciousness.

"So," I asked, "what is the problem? How can I help you?"

"Well," he replied, "this being tells me that I'm an avatar come to help humanity enter a new age. Is that true? He's offering to help me if it is."

This young man was sweet and had a number of good qualities, and I could see where he could be of service in any number of ways. I could also tell that he rather liked the idea of being an avatar, though he had no idea what that meant except that it promised power and a position where people would look up to him in admiration. The fact that a being would come out of the blue and lay such a responsibility on him was suspicious enough; the fact that his ego was becoming inflated by the idea rang all kinds of alarms. A little investigating on the inner confirmed for me what I suspected, that he had contacted a fairly low level being who was a genuinely negative entity in that it was seeking to parasitize him and feed on his subtle energy (and the energies of others whom he might attract as an "avatar") if he would let it fully into his life.

Such beings rarely attack directly. Like the old legends of vampires who have to be invited in before they can enter a victim's house, such beings cannot break through the natural subtle boundaries—the psychic immune system—that most people have around them. But as the great religions all testify in their wisdom, evil lures us with temptation more than it attacks us with force. Such entities attempt to appeal to our own greed and needs and to the lowest emotions with us, promising things that they have no intent upon delivering. This being knew how to talk a spiritual language and appeal to this young man's genuine desire to be of service; doing so, it hoped to be invited in, to seduce the young man with promises of significance and fame as a spiritual teacher.

Fortunately in this case, something in this young man—his soul or High Self, or perhaps an intervening Pit Crew member—created in him a sense of concern. Could he really be an avatar? It sounded farfetched. And what was an avatar anyway? These questions were what brought him to me, and in this case, he listened to what I had to say.

A less successful example occurred with a friend of mine who was also at times in touch with the subtle worlds. He was definitely drawn to power, a weakness he acknowledged and admitted to himself. But one day he called me to say he had had an opportunity to acquire and study a rare book on magic that dealt with invoking and controlling inner beings. In fact, he had already started testing it out and had made a contact with a very powerful being indeed. As he said this, I flashed in on this being's energy field and felt a presence of genuine darkness and evil. I warned my friend to drop it and leave it alone and shared with him what I'd seen. He assured me that he'd listen to me and would destroy the book.

I didn't hear from him for several months after that, and when I saw him next, he was not the same person I had known. He was fully in the thrall of a dark energy, and I knew immediately he had not listened to my advice but had gone ahead and invited this being into his life. At that point, there was nothing I could do, and he was no longer open to me as either a friend or a teacher in any event.

Not all beings whom we may experience as negative have a "pathology of identity" in which they have lost their connection to their own rootedness in the Sacred. We may simply be in the wrong place at the wrong time, creating a negative effect. If, when climbing in Arizona, I blindly put my hand in an opening in the rocks where a rattler might be living, and it then bites me, have I been attacked by a negative being or have I just been foolishly inattentive to my surroundings? From the rattler's point of view, I have just attacked it.

So it is possible to encounter beings who respond to us negatively but who are not themselves negative. An example might be a guardian entity who is protecting a boundary that we may have trespassed against. This might be inadvertent trespassing, but the guardian being doesn't necessarily know that. It is warning us away. I have found such beings around people occasionally but especially around places. Once I was walking on the grounds of a conference center where I was participating in a workshop. I came to a particular part of the estate and I got a very clear message, "Don't come in here." Visually it was just another part of the lawn, but it had an aura to it that was different—I don't know why. A guardian nature spirit arose and said, "Don't step into this area right now." So I turned back and walked away. I have no idea what was happening or why this guardian was there. Had I persisted in walking into that area, I am sure I would have felt an increasingly negative vibe. I might have felt the distress and anger of the nature spirits directed towards me.

A being might be angry and "negative" towards humans because of past hurts. I have encountered this with nature spirits from time to time in areas where the land has been despoiled or altered in a manner that disturbs or interferes with their work.

I live a few miles from a waterfall that is considered sacred by the local Native American tribes. It's a beautiful natural setting, so of course, developers came and built a resort complex with a hotel, shops, and restaurants right on a bluff overlooking the falls. One day I was walking in the woods near the river at the bottom of the falls when my attention was snagged by a nature spirit. It drew me into its consciousness, and at first, all I felt was a wonderful ecstasy and joy of life. This being was in touch with all the living plants around it, and through its eyes, I could see the streams of Light and life moving everywhere between these the plants. It was an amazing experience.

But then it drew me to a clearing from which I could see the waterfall and the resort lodge next to it at the top of the bluff. The whole energy of this nature spirit changed. I could see through its eyes that powerful currents of natural energy flowing through the land and particularly following the course of the river had been blocked or distorted by the buildings of the resort. The effect was a bit like someone upstream building a dam and preventing water from reaching the farmers downstream who needed it to irrigate their fields. It created a sensation akin to pain in this subtle being. As I stood there still enveloped in its consciousness, I felt an intense energy which I would have called fury had I felt it in myself or another human being. I could feel that this being wanted to destroy the lodge and wipe it off the face of the earth.

It was one seriously pissed off nature spirit!

I don't know if nature spirits and similar beings experience emotion in the same way or to the same degree that we do, but they certainly experience variations of energy that as far as I can tell act in the same way emotions do for us. The impression of rage may have been my human interpretation of what I was feeling, but there was no mistaking the intensity of the energy or the desire to see the lodge removed and proper flow restored to the local currents of subtle energy.

Going beyond nature spirits, within the planetary subtle realms one may find human spirits who are earthbound, as yet unwilling or possibly unable to move fully into the Post-Mortem Realms. Here, too, one may find human spirits that are not very advanced in understanding or development but who, because of strong attachments, have found a way back into contact with the incarnate world. In both cases, such individuals can seek to vent their distress or try to meet their emotional or mental needs through contact with a physical human being, at times masquerading as inner plane teachers or masters possessing much more wisdom or evolution than they really do in order to be accepted. They operate much like physical con artists, taking advantage of the needs or desires of the incarnate person whom they're contacting in order to exercise their will or gain some benefit.

Over the years I have had the opportunity to sit in on a number of sessions with different channels and other psychically sensitive people; at times as well, people come to me with messages they've received from some inner source and want my opinion of them. Unless a person is a student of mine and I'm responsible for his or her training, I make it a point not to comment on or criticize another sensitive's contacts or messages. Most people who ask me for such comments, I've discovered, really want me to affirm the high quality of their contact and its importance to the world; I learned through experience that they rarely want to hear what I actually have to say.

But the fact is that on many occasions the inner "teacher" with whom the individual is in contact is not very progressed at all and is simply enjoying the pleasure of being looked up to and regarded as someone special. Such a being is generally not negative or evil per se; it genuinely wishes to offer something good to its incarnate contacts, but it lacks real wisdom and is self-deluded, which unfortunately can foster self-delusion in the humans who believe in it.

Another possible dangerous area would be in the shadow domains of the Post-Mortem Realms. Here we find those individuals who died with violence and hatred in their hearts and minds and who are hopefully working their way clear into a more enlightened condition. Here, too, one may find those who died while in deep depression. On the whole these areas are veiled and sealed away from incarnate consciousness, which is true for much of the Post-Mortem Realms as I have already described. However, under the right circumstances, it is possible to penetrate those veils and find oneself in touch with one of these unfortunates, becoming exposed to the virulence of their particular negativity, whatever it may be. My understanding is that this is not an easy thing to accomplish and usually requires that the incarnate individual be in a state that's energetically equivalent and resonant with the conditions in one of these shadowlands. But there are times when drugs or alcohol, both of which can weaken or lower our psychic boundaries, particularly when used to excess, may open a door into one of these darker places

There are types of inner beings who are non-human who don't have anything like our emotions and who are by our standards amoral and impersonal. They can be disturbing to be around simply because they are so different, but they are not negative as such. They don't mean harm, though they might be harmful in inadvertent ways. An elephant can be harmful if I get in its way and it steps on me!

There is more that I could say, but I think I've said enough for you to get a picture of some of the dangers that exist in the subtle realms. As I said, I don't want to feed into the imagination of horrors and demonic entities waiting to possess and destroy us. There's enough of that already in the world, and the fear and mistrust such images produce are part of the reason the inner worlds are unable to form the kind of collaborative partnerships with us that can help heal the state of the world.

But having given you a list of negative things that you could run into, what are the things you can do to protect yourself. What is the equivalent in engaging with the inner worlds to my taking cool clothing, good hiking boots, and lots of water while hiking in the desert?

Of prime importance are personal awareness and an honest self-understanding and an attunement to the sacredness which is the root of your identity. If a person cannot own up to their own negativity, they may end up projecting it outwards, as I've said. It's not hard to indulge in denial about our own conflicted and negative sides; on the other hand, it's equally possible to be too harshly self-critical and judgmental. A balance of clear self-knowledge grounded in a loving, honoring attitude towards oneself, is what is needed.

Following this, your best preparation is through good energy hygiene and spiritual, moral hygiene. Your personal subtle field is your best line of defense, so you want to keep it energetically clean. This means a healthy lifestyle, exercise, rest, good diet, a generally positive outlook on life, and a practice of cultivating love, forgiveness, and goodwill in your relationships. It can mean finding an energetic connection with nature for the vitality in the natural environment can be powerfully restorative and cleansing to your own energy field. And it may mean cultivating a collaborative partnership with spiritual allies, particularly with your Pit Crew.

One thing that is very important is to do an inventory of your personal imaginal realm to see what negative, horrific, and fearful images may be there, particularly about the subtle worlds. Given all the frightening images modern media feeds us, it would be surprising if you don't have some of these thought-forms lurking in the back of your mind.

Such images do not serve you and, by making you fearful, can make you more vulnerable than you would otherwise be. So you want to get rid of them and replace them with more positive, empowering, loving images. You want to imagine that which honors your sovereignty and your sense of power and joy as a person and as a spiritual being. You want to be in touch with the generative processes that undergird your incarnation and produce your Self-Light, a process that is the focus of Incarnational Spirituality. And you want to stand in the Self-Light, that empersonal spirit and the light of your incarnation and engage with the subtle realms from that place of inner integrity and strength.

Getting angry now and then, having a good row, having an occasional depression, having a fit of jealousy, being fearful for a time, and so on, is NOT going to attract a negative entity all by itself unless you're in an environment where such critters have already been attracted and are present. Such negative emotions on our part need to be strong and persistent in us to attract an entity. We have to indulge in and express such negativity over a period of time so it becomes part of our habitual radiation. Then we can be seen by those who see such things, and what they will see is "food!"

You have protection from the Sacred who is the ultimate protection in all things. Call upon it if you feel the need. You have protection, if you call upon it, from your Pit Crew, from angelic beings, and most powerfully from your own soul, who has no desire at all to see its incarnational system compromised or invaded if it can prevent it—though this prevention needs to be invoked and acted upon by the personality as the incarnate agency.

Also, the best stance I've found towards negative energies is not to fight them or resist them but to make myself transparent and "Teflon-like" so they pass through and don't stick. I can also, by standing in my own inner Light, ask that they be transmuted as they pass through so that others won't be harmed. I ask my Pit Crew to always help me in this as well.

Finally, having a clear and definite process of discernment and integration—as well as a good buddy system—is important for avoiding or dealing with potential negative situations. I discuss all three in the next set of Field Notes.

Are there dangerous places in the subtle realms? Yes, but there are dangerous places in the world as a whole. Their existence doesn't mean that you have to run into them. For that matter, the street outside my home is dangerous if I cross it without paying attention when cars are going by. My home is filled with everyday, common appliances that could injure or kill me if I misuse them. If I stick my finger in a wall socket where it's not designed to go, I can expect a painful electrical shock. Safety lies in exercising awareness and common sense as well as a knowledge of the tools you have at hand. It's no different when engaging the subtle worlds.

Field Notes Eighteen:
Discernment

Discernment is critical in working with the subtle realms. This is not simply because an inner being may try to deceive us or because we may run into something harmful. It's also because we're opening ourselves to new sources of energy and information which we may never have encountered before. We may not be sure how to respond to or evaluate them. We have new responsibilities for the proper use of such information or energy in our lives. Sometimes we may feel overwhelmed. The most benign and loving being from the higher-order worlds may still misjudge how much energy we can absorb and integrate at one time, particularly when the contact is new and neither of you has much experience yet of the other. It may give us information we cannot use because it does not take into account the frailties or the limitations of incarnate life.

When John said that I had the right to say no to anything he asked of me, he was encouraging me to be discerning. After all, only I could know my limits in the moment, and while I might be able to transcend them at some point, to try to do so in that moment might lead to a breakdown rather than to a breakthrough.

So, discernment is not just for dealing with deception or evil. Discernment is a process of making wise choices in our life, of knowing what to do and what not to do, of what to accept and what not to accept. When confronted with obvious negativity, this choice can be easy (at least I hope it is!), but it's when we're confronted with choices for which there's no obvious right way or where all the choices seem equally good but lead to different consequences that discernment becomes challenging yet remains just as important. I knew, for instance, that John loved me and had only my best interests at heart. To decide to say no to something he had suggested was never an easy decision to make. It always required a real effort at discernment on my part.

As in many matters concerning the subtle worlds, you will develop your own unique ways of making discernments. That, after all, is what you do in your physical life, where you are making choices all the time about the people you associate with, the places you go, and the things you do. What are the criteria we use in our everyday choices? What values and ethics shape our discernments? Chances are many of those same criteria will apply to your inner contacts as well.

Often, discernment comes down to knowing yourself and trusting in your perceptions and intuitions, and this includes knowing your biases and weaknesses and the ways in which you may be led astray. It's based on self-knowledge and on developing knowledge of the new realms you're exploring.

Here are some things that have worked for me, which I'm glad to pass on: tools of the trade from one explorer to another.

The most important is to remember that you don't discern only with your mind. Discernment is not simply a mental exercise. You discern with your whole being, with your mind, your heart, your body, and your spiritual attunement. All aspects of you can come into play, and you want to pay attention to what your body says as a felt sense, for instance, as much as to an intuitive feeling or a logical insight.

Be proactive. The best time to fix a leaky roof is when the sun's shining before it starts to rain. If I wait to develop some discernment process until I actually need to be discerning, chances are I'll be too late. I won't have the foundation I need to make a good discernment.

So all discernment begins with the values and qualities, the integrity and standards, the knowledge, experience and wisdom we develop in ourselves as part of living. Specifically in this instance, discernment rests on a foundation of spiritual and moral practice and on a broad exercising of our mental faculties. It rests on our capacities to feel and sense deeply and to think clearly, both rationally and intuitively.

So practice discernment in all the regular, everyday parts of your life. Know yourself and where you stand in life spiritually, ethically, and in the use of your energy. Honor and love yourself and respect your boundaries.

A child can discern but he or she may make mistakes in such discernment because he or she has a limited base of experience and development on which to draw. Part of education—moral, spiritual, and cognitive is to give a child the tools and knowledge to make good choices as he or she gets older.

Inner discernment rests on the same principle. Seek out information about the inner worlds, ideally from a number of different authors and teachers so that you can get different perspectives. Each of us encounters the subtle worlds in our own way, which may be different from how you will do so. Be prepared to learn through experience, but take it gradually to give yourself time to assimilate and deepen your understanding.

We are at some disadvantage in our culture in that the inner worlds are generally branded as fantasy or non-existent, or as demon-haunted wastelands to be avoided at all costs, with the result that many people are "spiritually illiterate." The consequence of this either a lack of good information or distorted information and either can lead to bad discernment or no discernment at all. Many times over the years I've seen people accept inappropriate, mistaken and even hurtful information simply because it came from an inner being, and they felt that all inner beings must be wise and holy because they were "spiritual."

But even if you don't have ready access to more comprehensive information about the inner worlds, you still have access to a rich wisdom heritage in the various religious and spiritual traditions available to us. Likewise, in science, philosophy and the arts, we have traditions of using the intellect well. Just because you learn to use your mind well doesn't mean you will turn into a cynical skeptic. So by proactive discernment, I mean doing those things that strengthen your intellectual, moral, emotional, and spiritual character. Such practices, like the four practices that John gave me, build a strong and healthy energy field around you on many levels, and that field itself—like a good immune system—is your best insurance you will attract contacts that will honor your integrity and offer the best in a partnership. And as I said earlier in these Field Notes, the more you serve life itself and bring love and blessing into the lives of others, the more you resonate with the kind of higher-order beings you wish to contact.

Also, it helps to practice paying attention to subtle energies, such as those in a room or around objects, and developing your "energy senses." The more aware and alert you are to your subtle environment, the more that sensitivity will help you in evaluating the energies accompanying or radiating from a non-physical being. Remember, we are all energy systems. Being aware of that and taking it into account gives an important foundation for inner work.

Once a contact is made, you can begin a discernment process by paying attention to its energy—its "flavor" and radiance—and how that energy affects your own. With practice and patience (particularly if, as I just said, you practice with sensing the subtle emanations of the physical things in your environment), you can learn to feel and to discern the energy of inner beings, or at the very least, changes in your own energy caused by their presence.

One way that the subtle energy of a being manifests is through its effect on the "atmosphere" of the environment around you, as well as upon your own mood and state of being. When John would appear, people felt good in his presence. There was a sense of peace and of love that individuals could sense even if they weren't otherwise psychically sensitive. He created a good atmosphere.

The point is to pay attention to how you feel or respond energetically to a non-physical presence or force. If the energy field doesn't feel right to you, you may not wish to break off or reject the contact—you may wish more data—but it's an indication that all is not as it should be. This doesn't necessarily mean that the source of that energy is bad; it may simply be so different from your own that its field and yours initially have a hard time engaging or integrating. But it does mean that this contact is going to require work and discernment from you to make sure you both come away from it with a net gain in wholeness and benefits.

As I've said earlier, your body is one of your best allies in gauging energies and making discernments. If your body feels uncomfortable or is sending you signals of alarm (you might feel anxious, restless, tired, and so forth), that's something to pay attention to. Again, there could be different reasons for this other than the contact itself. Our mental and emotional states affect our body sensations, quite apart from any inner world contacts. We could genuinely be tired or restless. And any kind of inner world contact, even with the best and brightest of beings, can tire us. Dealing with the energy differences that accompany inner beings, particularly those from "upslope," is work, plain and simple. But, though the cause for a particular body reaction may not come from an inner contact, I still find it useful to pay attention to what my body's feeling and any sensations that may arise; it simply adds information I may use in my discernment process.

Also, as you begin working regularly with inner beings, the body may become a "signal system," contributing its bit to the vocabulary you develop between you. For instance, as I described in an earlier set of Field Notes, there is a place just above my right shoulder blade where I was once injured that gets tight and starts to hurt if I'm getting something wrong from the inner. If I misinterpret or don't read the energies correctly or am off base in some way, my shoulder begins to tighten and throb. It's an immediate and very specific physical signal that something's awry with the energies and I need to reconsider or reinterpret what's been coming from the inner.

You may well develop something similar in your body. The point is to see your body as an ally and to pay attention to its signals.

Another important tool for discernment is with our intellect. I think of this as cognitive discernment. I want to evaluate the information the being is giving me using the mental, emotional and intuitive tools at my disposal. I don't want either to reject it because I don't trust subtle beings and feel they probably don't exist anyway or accept it uncritically because it's coming from a subtle being and they are uniformly wiser and more knowledgeable than I am because they're from the realm of spirit. I want to consider the information and the contact as best I can as I would any person I met normally in my life and who had things to share with me.

Some of the questions I might ask myself (or even the contact) are:

- *Why do I want this information?*
- *How is this useful? What meaning does it have?*
- *How does it fit in with the spiritual and intellectual heritage of humanity?*
- *Does it make a difference or is it just "glamorous" information, "mind candy"? (For example, do I really need to know how many angels can dance on the head of a pin, or what the High Priest of the Sun Temple on Atlantis wore on his nights off, or how many crystals were on the altar of that Temple, or what the sexual practices of the natives of Alpha Centauri III might be? In other words, does it seduce me with the lure of ancient wisdom and hidden knowledge that only special people may know?)*
- *Is it in timing, that is, can the information be used or integrated in my life at this point in time?*

If possible, seek corroborating evidence. Pay attention in other aspects of your life. Sometimes discernment happens over time as new evidence becomes available, often synchronistically, or we see the effects and consequences of being engaged with a particular contact. If your life gets better as a result of a contact, that's useful information; if it falls apart and gets worse, that's useful information, too!

Of course, in asking questions like this, you need to keep in mind that not all information from the inner worlds can be evaluated according to everyday norms of rationality. Many subtle beings, particularly of the non-human variety such as nature spirits, simply don't think the way we do. And an inner being may indeed have access to information that we do not or that is not available on a physical level. For instance, some six years before it happened, John told me that a man named Gorbachev would become Premier of the Soviet Union and as a result of his leadership and actions, the Soviet Union would cease to exist. At the time he said this, I had no way of verifying such information and if anything, the Soviet Union seemed stronger than ever. But by then I had twenty years of experience with John and knew I could trust him. Two years later Gorbachev did indeed become Premier of the U.S.S.R and four years later the Soviet Union did fall apart just as John had said it would.

I have a general policy of treating most information from the inner worlds as hypotheses subject to further verification or evidence and subject to falsification. John's prophecy was just that, a hypothesis, at least until Gorbachev indeed was chosen to lead the U.S.S.R. Then it became more interesting and filled with new possibilities. (Even knowing and trusting John as much as I did, I would still have treated his statement as hypothesis since human free will and the play of circumstances could alter even the most trusted prophecy.)

When a message isn't clear, then I just wait. Usually it will come again in some other way, perhaps through a dream, perhaps through some form of synchronicity, perhaps another contact. I certainly do not understand everything that I pick up from the inner. If I don't know what to do with it or don't understand it, I can ask for clarification, but usually I just put it on the shelf. If nothing ever comes of it, well, life has its mysteries! It's like overhearing snatches of conversations in a crowded room or on a train or plane. I don't know the context or the meaning, and chances are I never will.

However, this is where a discipline like journaling can be handy. Writing things down, as in a dream journal, no matter how strange or disconnected the material may seem in the moment, can begin a process of connection and translation. Over time, it may make the messages clearer, and you may see connections that were not visible in the moment. Time, progression, sequence, logic—all these things are simply not the same on the inner as they are here. A message that was perfectly coherent in the mind of an inner contact may get distorted by the process of moving into our dimension and become clear only over a passage of time.

Another important form of discernment is peer review. Check out the information with people you trust, particularly if they have inner contacts themselves and understand the process. I have several close friends who are excellent sensitives engaging the subtle worlds in their own way; I frequently check with them about information I've received or contacts I've made to ask for their independent evaluation or for them to seek either confirmation or falsification of my information from their sources.

And if you feel you're being bothered by messages and contacts that make no sense and drain your energy, then that's when you say NO! and close the door. Tell the contact, "Come back again in a different way, or learn how to communicate properly with a human being!"

Even more important than intellectual discernment is that discernment based on your own character and sovereignty. This discernment asks questions like:

• How does this contact or message fit with my own wisdom and judgment or with common sense?
• How does it fit with my integrity? What is its impact on my wholeness and wellbeing?
• What consequences may follow from accepting it?
• How does this contact or information affect the integration and wholeness of my life?

If I'm going to take actions or accept information that creates disruption for myself or others, I need to have a good reason or be very trusting and sure of myself and my contact.

One point that John stressed in our partnership was the relationship of authority and responsibility when it came to consequences. "You cannot accept an idea or take an action based on my authority alone," he said. "You must take the authority, for you have the responsibility for what you believe or do. After all, in your world, it's you who must take the consequences for your actions, not me."

One danger of receiving information from the inner is the seduction of significance, the seduction of being special. The idea of receiving hidden wisdom from some "inner plane Master" can be heady and lead one to basking in reflected glory. After all, if a transcendent Being is sharing such pearls of wisdom with me, I must be pretty hot stuff myself!

To avoid this, I need to have a clear and honest understanding of my own needs and motives. If I have a need for recognition or to be special, then I need to make sure that that need doesn't influence either my inner contacts or the way I deal with what comes from them.

This brings up another area of discernment, which is the effect your contact with the subtle worlds may have on others and on your relationships and commitments.

Now, I don't necessarily mean here that I should be concerned if a contact discomfits some of my friends who may feel I've gone "round the bend" talking to invisible people. In our materialist culture, that would not be surprising. What I do mean is being aware and discerning about how the energy of a contact or the information it brings affects others through my own conduct. If I become ego-inflated, or less accountable and dependable, or too spacey, then this is going to affect those I'm close to. It can affect my ability to fulfill my commitments.

If I use my inner contact to limit or bind others to my will and ego and seek power over them because of my special inner plane associations, or I seek to make myself seem special or important in a manner that is deflating or detrimental to them, then I am walking a very thin line that can lead to pain and disaster. It is also the kind of behavior that can attract negative, mischievous or even evil beings from the darker corners of the lower subtle worlds.

Any inner contact that encourages me towards megalomania or messianic aspirations is highly suspect and in my view should be sent packing. The world needs good partners, not messiahs.

John provided me a good example here, for he was unfailingly respectful of my own identity and power and never tried to pull rank as a "superior spiritual being" or "inner plane master." He never told me to do anything, but if there was something he felt I should do, he presented it as a suggestion and left it to me whether to accept it or not. He was never demeaning in any way of my incarnate state or my humanity and dealt with me as a responsible adult in an adult partnership. I contrast this with some other contacts I've run across over the years that call (and treat) their human connections as "children" and never hesitate to let them know that as physical beings they occupy a lesser rank in the celestial hierarchy.

If a being offers information that pits one group against another, that encourages division and separation, or that inflames in any way, that is a suspect contact. Remember the object of the partnerships we form with inner contacts is enhance our ability to care, to nourish, to bless, and to create wholeness, not simply to deliver information and certainly not to promote conflict.

It's the energy that counts; it's presence that's important. Does the contact enhance your presence and energy, your love and compassion, your capacity to bless? Does it help you participate in the circle of your life and relationships more effectively and lovingly?

If after your best efforts at discernment, there remains a question about the reality, the rightness or the accuracy of the contact and the information or energy it may offer, put it "on a back burner" and let it be. It's better in the long run to honor your intellect, integrity and sovereignty and reject good information and a wise being than to give in and accept bad information or a slippery contact simply because you don't want to offend an inner being out of some false sense of reverence or hierarchy, or because of the glamour of "working with inner forces."

These are just a few ideas that I have found helpful in my own discernment processes. There are so many possible kinds of experiences and so many different ways that people may exercise discernment in response to them that all I can do here is skim the surface of the possibilities. As with so many aspects of engaging the subtle worlds, in the end you have to find what works for you, keeping in mind your overall objectives. One thing to keep in mind, as I mentioned in an earlier set of Field Notes: every contact has an immediate, short-term effect but it also takes place in the larger contexts of your life as a whole and the ongoing great work of the spiritual realms to create planetary wholeness. If you keep that longer and larger context in mind as part of your discernment, it will help immensely.

Field Notes Nineteen: Integration

Integration is what you do after discernment has taken place. Integration is how you bring the content of your contact with the subtle worlds into your life and make it part of your everyday world. As with discernment, I can only give you some "rules of thumb" here, since each person is different and will integrate the elements of such a contact into her or his life in unique ways.

By integration, I mean that the energy and information that constitutes the "meat" of partnership with an inner being becomes part of your life in a useful and nourishing way. It adds to your life, or at least doesn't detract from it or make it less coherent in the long run.

One of the things you may need to integrate is information. Inner contacts can give us various kinds of information. Some of it may pertain to events and people in our daily lives; some of it may be esoteric, philosophical and cosmological; some of it may be about ourselves. One kind of information that many people seek from inner contacts is guidance or advice.

All information has to be vetted through whatever discernment process you may use. Is it accurate? Is it useful? Is it meaningful? Is it good? Is it true or just imaginary and fanciful? But once the information has passed your tests of discernment, then what do you do with it?

It depends, of course, on the nature of the information. Some information simply needs to be acted upon. In the summer of 1970, John suggested that I go to Europe to find the place where I would begin my next cycle of work. I did, and I ended up at Findhorn where I worked as a co-director of the community for three years.

Sometimes the information asks for changes in your life. If, for instance, an inner being tells you it would be better for you to be a vegetarian for awhile, then integrating that information would involve learning about a vegetarian diet, shopping and cooking differently, enduring the cravings for meat that may arise, making sure you have a healthy and balanced diet without animal protein, and so forth. You may wish to find out why such a diet is being recommended. Is it for physical health reasons? Is it for ideological or spiritual reasons? Do you go along with those reasons?

Learning and gaining wisdom is an important form of integrating information. Sometimes that's all that's needed. You have added to your store of knowledge and understanding about the world. But sometimes the information requires something more. It might be information about yourself. If you decide the information is correct, then what do you do about it? How do you make it part of your life?

I once visited a friend of mine who was a channel. As I came up to his house, a woman stormed out, very angry. When I went in, he explained she was a client, and he had just given her a reading. "She's been to me several times before," he said. "She has a problem believing in herself and getting on with her life. So this time Gordon [his inner plane contact whom he channeled for clients] simply told her she was hopeless, that she had no hope of ever progressing spiritually, that she was failing in this life, and would never amount to anything. Basically he let her have it. That's why she got so angry. She shouted at him that he was wrong and she would prove it!" He smiled. "That's exactly the reaction Gordon was hoping for. He wanted to get her so angry at him that she would be energized to prove him wrong and thus get out of the stuck place she's in. Nothing else has seemed to work."

This was an interesting strategy, and I hope it worked for the lady. But look at it from her point of view. She received information from what to her was a respected and powerful inner source that her life had no meaning, that she was hopeless, and she would never amount to anything spiritually. How does she integrate that information? One way, the way that my friend hoped she would take, would be to reject it and in so doing spur herself on to take the necessary efforts to improve her life. But there's a risk here. She might integrate the information by agreeing with it and becoming even more despondent and stuck.

Or suppose you've been told by an inner being that you were in a past life a particular historical personage like Napoleon? How do you integrate information like this? In one way it doesn't matter. You are who you are today, and that's what puts potatoes on the plate and love in your heart. Such information runs risks as well. You could identify with that personage in inappropriate ways; you could become egoistically inflated. Or you might feel depressed, wondering how you can measure up to the past (assuming it was as noble life) or live it down (assuming it wasn't).

On the other hand, the pattern of that past life might throw light on patterns you're experiencing now, which could be useful in transforming your present experience and bringing healing into your life.

The effects of the energy differential between yourself and an inner contact may also need to be integrated. These effects can leave you feeling high and elated, or they can lead to a crash and depression due to the fatigue of dealing with that difference. As I've said, working with inner beings is just that, work.

Any new experience—new information, new insights, or new energies—can cause temporary and localized disruption. The fact that you might be thrown off stride for a day or two, or even a week or a month is not a big deal in the larger flow of your life. For example, sometimes after a particularly intense "download" of information or energy from the inner worlds, it may take me a day or two to get my energy back to normal. I'm accustomed to this and know the symptoms (I get a bit "spacey" and sometimes fatigued, like after a hard day of physical labor). It's no big deal and has no longer term effect. If I need to, I can shrug it off and do whatever the day requires of me, but if I can, I usually rest or do something different on such days.

At Findhorn, when someone felt overwhelmed by "the energies," we would have them work in the garden or hug a tree or in some way make contact with the earth as a grounding technique. Physical exercise itself is almost always helpful.

Integration may involve others. Using the earlier example of following guidance to become a vegetarian, if you're married and have a family, how will that affect your spouse and children? How can they help you be a vegetarian? How can you avoid disrupting their lifestyle too much if they don't wish or need to join you?

Another level of integration is how your contact affects your relationship to your society. A very negative and horrific example of this are those people who feel they've received "guidance" to kill or harm someone else. A positive example would be someone who has an inner contact that transforms him or her into a compassionate and loving person, or someone who gets inner direction to do volunteer work or to give service in a particular way. This is what happened to Scrooge in Dickens's Christmas fable.

Ultimately, I believe that the function of integration is to make yourself more whole, your relationships more whole, your society more whole.

Field Notes Twenty:
Buddies

When I was a child living on the American air base at Nouasseur in Morocco, I went one day with a friend to the base swimming pool. I didn't know yet how to swim, but I would put my head in the water, close my eyes (because the chlorine in the pool made them sting), and just head out kicking and splashing. I was supposed to be "swimming" across the width of the pool at the shallow end where I could stand up if I got into trouble, but at one point I got turned around and headed off into the deep end by mistake.

With my eyes closed, I had no idea where I was going, but I realized that it was taking me longer than usual to get to the other side of the pool. So I decided to stand up and look around. Of course, my feet didn't find the bottom of the pool as it was three feet below me, and I began to sink. I actually began to drown, and I remember looking up at the top of the water some two feet above me, seeing the sun sparkling beautifully on the its surface, and feeling very peaceful as I bobbed around the bottom. Then strong hands grabbed me and pulled me out and got me onto the side of the pool where I began to cough up all the water that had gotten into my lungs. My friend had looked around and not seen me, then realized I had sunk to the bottom of the deep end and called to an adult to fish me out.

All was well and my life was saved, but I could have been in real trouble had I not had my friend with me. It reinforced what my mother and others had always told me: if you're going swimming, don't go alone. Take a buddy.

This is excellent advice for working with the subtle worlds, too. It's such excellent advice, in fact, that I want to give it its own set of Field Notes.

The buddy system I have in mind isn't exactly for journeying into the subtle worlds, though that is possible through shared meditations and the like. What I have in mind is really part of the discerning and integration process. It has elements of a peer review, but it doesn't depend on finding someone who also is exploring or has experience with the subtle worlds.

Your buddy or "soul friend" doesn't necessarily have to have inner contacts. Sometimes it may be better if they don't. The main requirements are that they can listen to you respectfully without judgment, that they can be a sounding board as you share what experiences or material you may have received, and that they can reflect back to you with honesty. What you want in this reflection is not their opinion on whether the information or contact is real or not, but a sense of its impact, consequence, and meaning in your life. You want them to help you think it through.

Inner contacts by their nature, as I have described earlier, can generate a powerful energy that can sweep you along, make clear evaluation difficult. You can feel an emotional and energetic "high" in which both the contact and whatever you have received from it are enveloped in a halo effect. Your buddy, however, will not be feeling that and therefore is in a good position to give you a clearer perspective on it than you may be able to have in the moment.

If you have received information or a message, ask your buddy to repeat or paraphrase it back to you. Having a buddy give you the same information in his or her words gives you a chance to hear it from an ordinary human being rather than a being from some other glamorous other realm and thus see if it carries the same "charge" or impact for you. Freed from the halo of the contact itself, such information can often seem much more mundane and ordinary—and less important—than when you experienced it within the energetic field of the inner worlds. It's easier then to evaluate and integrate it.

Remember, the role of the buddy is not—at this point at least—to give an opinion *about* the information or the contact, only to reproduce it in a different context. Again you are using the power of difference to gain a deeper insight.

You can also ask your buddy to reflect honestly on what he or she thinks of the information. What is his or her opinion of it or of the contact? This can be helpful, too. But here you want to be sure that your buddy isn't just giving a knee-jerk response based on his or her own biases. A person who will always tell you to leave subtle beings alone because they're dangerous or who will always tell you how wonderful it is—and you are—to have such amazing contacts is not performing the role of a buddy here.

A buddy is there to reflect your experience back to you through the eyes, ears and mind of an empathetic and sympathetic listener and friend. Your buddy should be someone who knows you fairly well and can let you know if they feel the information is affecting or changing you in ways you may not see clearly. Such a change might well be for the better, which is good, but it might be accentuating parts of your personality that are not so nice, such as an ego-based need for power or for feeling special. Being called out on that by a buddy you trust can help you maintain integrity and psychological balance.

Often just talking with someone can help integrate an experience. Writing and journaling can do the same, but they lack the interactive element you have with a buddy.

Finally, here's another rule of thumb I have. I regularly wait three days before acting on inner information (or trying to evaluate it) if I can. This gives time for the energy of the contact to settle down so I can more easily evaluate the information itself. If I can't find a buddy to help, this can serve as well.

Remember what I wrote about the cognitive imagination in an earlier set of Field Notes. Taking time can also be important because inner information often comes in such a condensed, hieroglyphic manner that it needs time to be unpacked or, like seeds, to unfold in my understanding. If I'm not sure about information I've received or what to do with it, I wait three days and usually either something else will happen that clarifies it or I've had time to "unpack" it.

The inner worlds often have to communicate with us through the images we provide. It can be a bit like playing charades. We have to discern what is being said and we can't take the surface impression of the communication literally. There is the famous example of St. Francis who was told in a vision by Jesus to "rebuild My church." In the long run, it is apparent that this meant the Church as a whole institution by giving it new inspiration and example, but in the moment, Francis took it literally and set about rebuilding a specific church that had fallen into ruin by begging for and collecting stones.

Or a message that "you are going through a death process," may simply mean that many things are changing in your life and you are transforming, not that you are about to exit physical incarnation.

Having a buddy to reflect with you upon the images and ideas contained in a message can be important as the buddy may be less inclined to accept what you saw or heard at face value. If the buddy can ask good questions, and you're willing to entertain them, then much can be unpacked that otherwise might go misunderstood or unnoticed. As in many things, two eyes and two heads are often better than one.

The subtle worlds are like a vast ocean of information and meaning. Having a buddy to help when you go 'swimming' in it makes it a safer experience all the way around.

Field Notes Twenty-One:
Subtle Activism

Subtle activism takes advantage of the fact that we live in three worlds at once, the physical world, the subtle energetic fields of the planet that correspond to our own personal subtle "bodies," and the subtle worlds themselves. In the metaphor I've been using in these Field Notes, these make up the land, the seashore, and the ocean, and we belong to all three.

Physical activism is when we take helpful actions in the physical world to make the world a better place. Subtle activism is when we do the same thing but acting within the subtle fields of the planet with help from the inner worlds themselves. In my metaphor, we're wading in the water at the beach to gain resources from the ocean that can help problems on the land.

There are many different forms that subtle activism can take. The topic as a whole is broader than I can cover here. In my educational work, it constitutes a class all on its own. But I mention it as part of these Field Notes for it gives meaning to why we would wish to engage with the subtle worlds at all.

One way we can perform subtle activism is through the interaction of our own personal subtle fields through intention, love, and imagination with the subtle fields of the planet, or more specifically of those particular places on the planet where help is needed. It is not a substitute for physical activism, but often when there is a problem on one level, there are corresponding problems on several other levels as well. Thus, when an earthquake strikes a city, there is physical devastation, injuries and loss of life, all of which need tending by physical aid workers and rescuers. But the pain, the suffering, and the mental and emotional anguish also roil the subtle fields connected to that city and there may other unbalanced energetic effects as well related to the earth, to the nature in the area, and so on. Physical aid cannot address these issues, yet unless they are addressed, wholeness and healing will be slower in returning to that area.

This is where a subtle activist can help make a difference. He or she, drawing on his or her resources of love, compassion, and other good energies, can broadcast those qualities into the subtle field of the city, helping to change its overall energy vibration. As time and space do not act as boundaries in the subtle worlds, a person can do this from anywhere in the world. In effect, this is what prayer groups have done for centuries. Training in subtle activism simply adds the additional skills based on knowledge of one's personal subtle field, one's generative incarnational processes, and the nature and character of the planet's subtle dimensions.

However, there is a limit to what a person can do or should attempt to do all on his or her own. This is where partnership with allies from the transitional and higher-order realms really comes into its own. Subtle activism is one of the positive fruits of all the work, training and energy spent in engaging with the inner worlds and developing collaborative alliances with appropriate and helpful subtle beings.

Through such partnerships, the energy, presence and wisdom of the non-physical partner can be added, often with great affect, to the presence and energy of the incarnate individual. Using my metaphor, imagine standing in the seashore trying to move a heavy log and then having a powerful wave sweep in from the ocean and add its kinetic energy to your own. Chances are good that log will be picked up and moved!

The physical world is our responsibility. But the subtle worlds are home ground to our spiritual allies. And there are many beings who could be our allies in specific situations: the spirits of a place (like the angel overlighting the city that suffered the earthquake, or the deva overlighting the surrounding environment), human-oriented elementals and angels, servers from the Post-Mortem Realms—the list could go on and on. We do not lack for potential partners.

Many higher-order beings may wish to help humanity and alleviate suffering but are unable to do so directly. After all, the suffering is physical but they are non-physical, and they may be too far "upslope" energetically to effectively connect. But if a human being becomes a subtle activist, does what's necessary to move partly upslope himself or herself so contact can be made and energies exchanged, then in the partnership that ensues, the higher-order beings have a way of making their blessing and positive energies available to the physical world. The subtle activist becomes their hands and feet.

Subtle activism can also respond to initiatives being taken on the inner to help humanity. At one point during the Iraq war, for example, I was seeking to do some subtle activism for Baghdad which was suffering a great deal of violence at the time. As I tuned into the city, I was surprised to see that a dome of Light had appeared in the subtle realms above and around the place. This dome was radiating not only loving energies into the surrounding area but also calming and soothing ones, trying to dampen down the "hot" passions of anger and hatred that were roiling the local subtle environment. In effect, this dome was seeking to contribute to the emergence of peace in the city.

As I drew closer, I saw that the dome was being fed and energized by a variety of beings, but chief among them were soldiers and fighters from both sides, Americans and insurgent Iraqis, who had been killed in the fighting. Rather than moving on into the Post-Mortem Realms immediately, they had chosen to stay behind and to use their closeness to the physical world—having so recently left it—as a form of connection to the minds and hearts of the people in the city. The whole thing was being organized in fact by a young woman who had been an aid worker in Baghdad and who had also recently been killed. She was obviously a powerful soul in order to begin such a project so soon after entering the subtle worlds and to attract the help she needed. In effect, she was continuing the healing and peace-making work she'd been doing while in the physical body.

As I approached, I was contacted by one of the angelic beings working with the dome and asked if I could add energy to it, which

I was honored to do. And they were actively seeking out other physical individuals who were sensitive enough to see or sense what was happening and who could add needed energies from our side to help in this project. It was like they were building a sand castle in the shallow water of the beach but needed people to carry sand from the land to reinforce and strengthen the structure to make sure the whole thing didn't get washed away.

This is also a form of subtle activism.

A third form of subtle activism to which I alluded in an earlier set of Field Notes is partnering with spiritual allies to do energy hygiene and to help clean up energetically toxic subtle atmospheres in the world around us. This is particularly useful when dealing with the Imaginal realm, but it can be important anywhere within the subtle energy fields of the earth that negative energies are blocking the circulation of spiritual energies.

As I said, this is a much larger topic than I can elaborate upon here. Subtle activism doesn't have to be used just for problems in the world. It can be used to enhance inspiration, to support good things going on or just to provide blessings. When it is linked with partnerships forged with spiritual allies, then it becomes very powerful. Then it represents the best of what engaging with the subtle worlds is all about.

Field Notes Twenty-Two: For the Road

We come to the end. As we do, I realize that full as these Field Notes may seem, they only scratch the surface. For that matter, after sixty years, I feel I've only scratched the surface myself. As I said in the beginning, there is much I did not include because some things need to be shared in a different context. There's a reason why many spiritual teachings and insights were traditionally passed on only orally or in a manner that allowed for interaction. It's not that that information is secret, only that it is not easily reducible to words and is best passed on through experiential means or where questions can be asked and answered. And also there is much that only you can discover in your own way for yourself.

And there's much I didn't include because I'm still exploring and researching. This is truly a lifetime endeavor.

My object, as I have said, is to provide a simple introduction to the idea of the subtle worlds and the beings upon them, as well as to the idea of collaborative partnerships between the two halves of the planet's total ecology. We are in a time of great challenge to humanity and to our capacity to become a true planetary species, capable of creating wholeness and blessing throughout the planet. I am assured by my inner colleagues that this is possible, and I believe this is so. But we need to take steps to make it so. One of those steps, I believe, is to gain a new understanding of the subtle worlds and learn how to work with them in collaboration.

This means at the least coming to an understanding of who we are as beings of both spirit and earth, able to bridge between the physical earth and the higher-order worlds, something I explore in my teachings in Incarnational Spirituality. It also means rising above our fears and misconceptions of the non-physical worlds and their denizens, a goal to which I hope this book contributes.

For some years now, scientists have been exploring meditation and the relationship of science to internal transpersonal states by working in collaboration with trained and powerful meditators. My dream is that we come to a time when we put the same kind of attention and collaboration towards the reality of the subtle worlds and the work that is possible in partnership with them. The scientist in me would delight in that happening, even as the mystic and subtle activist in me sees it as a necessity.

The Findhorn Foundation community, of which I was a co-director for three years in the early Seventies, began exploring this in its work of cooperation with nature spirits and devas in the growing of a miraculous garden in inhospitable soil. But much still needs to be done to follow up on that initial pioneering work. The work that was done holds out promise for a program of dedicated scientific and mystical research.

There are a lot of cultural norms that are violated by seeking out and working with the subtle worlds and spiritual allies. Most Western religions have a tradition of caution and warning about such endeavors, if not outright prohibition, while in the East, though there is more acceptance of this phenomenon, it is often seen as a detriment and obstacle to realizing the pure truth of Beingness. And of course, Western materialistic science and psychology flatly declare the kind of experiences that I have and others like me to be delusional nonsense.

Further it takes work and training to do this kind of thing well. It can mean sacrifices of time and energy and a discipline of self-reflection and monitoring to make sure one stays "on the beam" and in harmony. The impact of the energies of the subtle worlds upon one's personal subtle body, not to mention one's mind and emotions, can be tiring and challenging at times and requires a discipline of inner work to maintain balance. There have been moments when I've thought of just chucking it all out the window!

But the compensations are well worth it. For one thing, you begin to realize just what it means to be a human being and to be incarnated on this planet: the joy of it, the wonder of it, the blessing of it. There is the satisfaction of serving to create wholeness, and there is the sheer delight of sensing the ecstasy that runs under everything as the very essence of life itself. In addition there is the sense of belonging that comes from seeing everything in the world as alive and yourself as part of it.

I would not trade my twenty-seven years of partnership with John for anything, nor would I give up the partnerships I have now with various inner colleagues. It hasn't always been easy by any means, but I am a better person for it, a better husband, a better father, and, I trust, a better human being.

So would I recommend engaging with the subtle worlds? Yes, as long as you go into it with your eyes open and with a willingness to be changed and challenged in many ways. It is an adventure into love: love for self, love for others, love for the world, love for the Sacred. And if you go far enough along this path, it will demand that you become a force for wholeness in yourself and in the world. If that sounds good, then I hope this book will be a stepping stone on your way.

With that, I leave you with my deepest blessings and with this final thought for the road ahead.

Whatever other purposes partnership with the subtle worlds may fulfill, there is one grand objective: to bring forth a time when we will experience the earth not as two worlds, one physical and one non-physical, but as one united planet of sacred life and consciousness, singing a song of wholeness to the stars and taking its place as a radiance of love and blessing for all the universe.

Resources

If this book has stimulated your interest and you would like to explore further, here are some resources to help you do so.

CLASSES

I teach classes on the material in these Field Notes, adding to and going beyond the material I've presented here. These classes, most of which are taught online over the Internet or through a combination of online and face-to-face gatherings, allow a chance for interaction and experiential learning, which as I've said in the Field Notes, I consider important.

Our program is always evolving as the research into Incarnational Spirituality and the work with the subtle worlds evolves. Long-term studies can lead to a Masters Degree in Contemporary Spirituality. For information about what classes and programs are currently available, please go to our website, www.Lorian.org.

SELF-DIRECTED STUDY MODULES

Lorian also offers a line of self-directed study modules on a variety of topics such as energy hygiene, subtle activism, and incarnational spirituality. Again, to see what is available, please go to our website, www.Lorian.org.

BOOKS

Along with classes and self-directed study modules, I also write books like this one. To see what is currently available, please go to our bookstore at the Lorian website. (Please note that the book that describes my training with John in some detail, *Apprenticed to Spirit*, by Riverhead Books, has been delayed in publication but hopefully will be out sometime in 2010.)

There are a number of excellent authors whose work

complements these Field Notes or who offer material (as with psychic protection) that goes beyond what I do. Here is a selection of them.

Experiences with the Dying and the Dead, by Claire Blatchford; Lindisfarne Books, 2007.

(An excellent and beautifully written book about life after death, the journey into the Post-Mortem Realms, and the experiences of those post-mortem people who return to partner with the living.)

Feeling Safe, by William Bloom; Piatkus Books, 2002.

Psychic Protection: Creating Positive Energies for People and Places, by William Bloom; Fireside, 1997.

(These two books by William Bloom are excellent books for dealing with negative energies and creating positive energies for oneself and others. I recommend them all the time to my classes.)

The Endorphin Effect, by William Bloom; Piatkus, 2001.

(William is one of the best teachers I know in the area of subtle energy dynamics, and this book is one of his best, giving a wealth of insights and exercises for creating positive energy within oneself using the body as an ally.)

Meeting Fairies: My Remarkable Encounters with Nature Spirits, by R. Ogilvie Crombie; Allen and Unwin, 2009.

(Crombie was the remarkable Scotsman who was the primary contact for the Findhorn community with the nature spirits; his experiences and his eloquent way of relating them give great insight into working with these denizens of the subtle worlds. I highly recommend it.)

The Living Universe, by Duane Elgin; BK Publishers, 2009.

(This is an outstanding new book for communicating one of the basic teachings of the inner worlds: that the universe itself and everything in it is alive. Elgin, a scientist and mystic, takes a scientific approach to this theme that is elegant and persuasive. Excellent.)

Testimony of Light, by Helen Greaves; Tarcher, 2009.

(This is a remarkable and excellent book detailing the Post-Mortem Realms (or at least one aspect of them). It chronicles the experiences of a remarkable woman who because of a telepathic link she established with a friend during her life is able to give a report on her experiences after her death.)

On Becoming an Alchemist, by Catherine MacCoun; Trumpeter Books, 2008.

(This is one of my favorite books and one of the best I've read on spirituality and in particular on dealing with the subtle realms and the beings upon them. Witty and knowledgeable, it belongs on every spiritual worker's bookshelf.

Psychic Shield, by Caitlin Matthews; Ulysses Press, 2006.

(Caitlin is an outstanding spiritual teacher and shamanic practitioner. She brings her knowledge, wisdom and experience to what might be called a "street-smart" book on dealing with negative subtle energies and unpleasant beings, as well as on ways to keep your energy field healthy and vital.)

The Sidhe: Wisdom from the Celtic Otherworld, John Matthews; Lorian Press, 2004.

(This is an excellent introduction to the Sidhe from an outstanding teacher and shamanic practitioner; based on his own experiences, this is a story of contact with the Sidhe told by a man who is a true "walker between the worlds.")

The Only Three Things: Tapping the Power of Dreams, Coincidence and Imagination, Robert Moss; New World Library, 2007.

(Robert is an experienced walker of the inner worlds and has a number of fine books out detailing his experiences and insights; I choose this one for this list because of its discussion of the importance of the imagination in spiritual work, though everything he says here is valuable.)

Unseen Worlds and Practical Aspects of Spiritual Discernment, Anastacia J. Nutt; R.J.Stewart Books, 2008.

(I discovered this book while working on my own Field Notes and discovered a lot of parallels. It is well written and filled with Anastacia's insights, practical experience, and compassionate consciousness. Her discussion of discernment is excellent.)

Soul Companions, Edited by Karen Sawyer; O Books, 2008.

(This book contains the stories of 45 different individuals, each of whom is working with the subtle worlds and non-physical allies in their own unique way. This is an excellent book for giving an insight into the various forms contact with the subtle worlds can take in the lives of different people and yet there are definite threads of commonality that run through all of them.)

The Living World of Faery, R.J. Stewart; RJStewart Books, 2003.

(R. J. Stewart is one of the finest teachers and scholars in the Celtic tradition and the folklore of the Faery Traditions, a man who also speaks and writes from the depth of personal experience as an explorer between the worlds.)

Meditation as Contemplative Inquiry: When Knowing Becomes Love, by Arthur Zajonc; Lindisfarne Books, 2009.

(This is an excellent book that presents an approach to meditation and knowledge of the inner worlds that is very close to what I learned from my mentor John, emphasizing the role of love in the gaining of insights. Written by a quantum physicist who has his own practice of contact with the subtle worlds, it demonstrates a rare blending of science and spirituality. I recommend it highly.)

MEDIA

Flatland: The Movie; starring Martin Sheen, Kristen Bell, Michael York; Flat World Productions, 2008.

(The book Flatland written in 1884 by Edwin Abbot is a classic, offering a remarkable depiction of transdimensional contact and the confusion it can create as a three-dimensional sphere attempts to communicate with a two-dimensional square. This movie delightfully animates this story and gives a beautiful depiction of the challenges and transformations that occur when a higher dimensional being and a lower-dimensional one strike up a partnership. It captures very well many of the challenges that occur when an incarnate human in our 3-D world and a hyperdimensional being from the higher-order worlds come together. I often use this DVD movie in my classes to illustrate this point, which it does much better than I can just talking about it.)

Other books by
David Spangler

Blessing: *The Art and the Practice*

The Call

Parent as Mystic - Mystic as Parent

Manifestation: *Creating the life you love*

Everyday Miracles

The Story Tree

The Incarnational Card Deck and Manual

The Flame of Incarnation

Textbook Series

World Work

Crafting Home: *Generating the Sacred*

Space-Crafting: *The Holding of Self*

Crafting Relationships: *The Holding of Others*

Crafting Inner Alliances: *The Holding of Spirit*

Incarnational Spirituality: *A strategy to Bless our World*

About the Author

David Spangler lives in the Northwest, is married and has four children. He has been a spiritual teacher since 1964. From 1970-1973, he was a co-director of the Findhorn Foundation Community in Northern Scotland. In 1974 he co-founded the Lorian Association, a non-profit spiritual educational organization, and continues to work with it today. David is also a Fellow of the Lindisfarne Association, a gathering of scientists, mathematicians, artists, spiritual and religious teachers, ecologists, and political scientists, all interested in promoting a new culture based on holistic and Gaian values. For further information on his work, writings and classes, please visit www.lorian.org.

About the Publisher

Lorian Press is a private, for profit business which publishes works approved by the Lorian Association. Current titles by David Spangler and others can be found on the Lorian website.

The Lorian Association is a not-for-profit educational organization. Its work is to help people bring the joy, healing, and blessing of their personal spirituality into their everyday lives. This spirituality unfolds out of their unique lives and relationships to Spirit, by whatever name or in whatever form that Spirit is recognized.

For information, go to www.lorian.org, email info@lorian.org, or write to:

The Lorian Association
P.O. Box 1368
Issaquah, WA 98027

Praise for
Subtle Worlds: An Explorer's Field Notes

"There are so many books on the subject of spirit communication, published over the last 150 years, that we might seriously ask why do we have yet another one from David Spangler? Here is why: David writes from direct experience, not theory. Significantly he has by-passed all the usual spiritualist and New Age dogma repeated in countless books and courses and offers us instead a direct and clear approach. The subject is presented in the only truly effective way, by comparing the inner spiritual realms to our interactions in the mundane world. Thus we have a text filled with inspiration, insights, and inestimably valuable doses of common sense. I recommend this book highly, and will be encouraging my own students to study it."

R J Stewart, author of *Merlin: The Prophetic Vision and Mystic Life, The Sphere of Art, The Dreampower Tarot*, and many others

"This is a wonderful book--warm, wise, engaging, and profound. I can't imagine a better introduction to the dimensions of inner experience."

Richard Smoley, author of *The Dice Game of Shiva: How Consciousness Creates the Universe*

"These are the field notes of an ambassador as well as an explorer. The knowledge that we're connecting with the subtle worlds all the time, everywhere, in every direction, wherever we are, as we evolve and it evolves, is at the heart of David's journey. And, as you'll discover in this book, he's a creative, generous, and tireless worker in the name of partnership and love."

Claire Blatchford, author of *Experiences with the Dying and the Dead*